Drumming Our Way Home

Georgina Martin

Drumming Our Way Home

Intergenerational Learning, Teaching, and Indigenous Ways of Knowing

© UBC Press 2024

All rights reserved. No part of this publication may be reproduced, stored in a retrieval system, or transmitted, in any form or by any means, without prior written permission of the publisher, or, in Canada, in the case of photocopying or other reprographic copying, a licence from Access Copyright, www.accesscopyright.ca.

Printed in Canada on FSC-certified ancient-forest-free paper (100% post-consumer recycled) that is processed chlorine- and acid-free.

UBC Press is a Benetech Global Certified Accessible™ publisher. The epub version of this book meets stringent accessibility standards, ensuring it is available to people with diverse needs.

Library and Archives Canada Cataloguing in Publication

Title: Drumming our way home : intergenerational learning, teaching, and Indigenous ways of knowing / Georgina Martin.

Names: Martin, Georgina (Georgina Rose), author.

Description: Includes bibliographical references and index.

Identifiers: Canadiana (print) 20240441877 | Canadiana (ebook) 20240443357 | ISBN 9780774870085 (hardcover) | ISBN 9780774870092 (softcover) | ISBN 9780774870108 (PDF) | ISBN 9780774870115 (EPUB)

Subjects: LCSH: Martin, Georgina (Georgina Rose) | LCSH: Experiential learning. | LCSH: Intergenerational relations. | LCSH: Identity (Psychology) | CSH: Secwépemc —Biography. | CSH: Secwépemc—Social life and customs. | LCGFT: Autobiographies.

Classification: LCC E99.S45 M37 2024 | DDC 305.897/943—dc23

UBC Press gratefully acknowledges the financial support for our publishing program of the Government of Canada, the Canada Council for the Arts, and the British Columbia Arts Council.

This book has been published with the help of a grant from the Canadian Federation for the Humanities and Social Sciences, through the Scholarly Book Awards, using funds provided by the Social Sciences and Humanities Research Council of Canada.

UBC Press is situated on the traditional, ancestral, and unceded territory of the xʷməθkʷəy̓əm (Musqueam) people. This land has always been a place of learning for the xʷməθkʷəy̓əm, who have passed on their culture, history, and traditions for millennia, from one generation to the next.

UBC Press
The University of British Columbia
www.ubcpress.ca

In honour of my Ancestors and grandparents,
xpé7e Ned and kyé7e Nancy Moiese.

To Pat, Kirsten, Trevor, and Melissa:
Thank you for your thoughts and unwavering support.

For my son Kyle (1987–2023) and daughter Denise (1974–2022):
You continue to inspire me.
May you both keep soaring on the wings of eagles.

Contents

List of Illustrations / ix

Secwépemc Prayer / x

Foreword / xi
Jo-ann Archibald Q'um Q'um Xiiem

Preface / xv

CHAPTER 1
Drumming as Metaphor / 3

CHAPTER 2
The Drum Reverberates against the Intergenerational Aspects of Colonialism / 26

CHAPTER 3
Honouring the Drummer: Embodied Knowledge from within My Community / 48

CHAPTER 4
Elder Jean's Stories: Passing the Drum Forward to the Next Generation / 74

CHAPTER 5
Colten's Stories: Memories and Values / 100

CHAPTER 6
Intergenerational Knowledge Transmission / 121

Notes / 133

References / 135

Index / 138

List of Illustrations

1.1 Ned and Nancy Moiese, Georgina's grandparents / 6
1.2 Map of Secwépemc Territory / 12
1.3 Relational sphere depicting the connections between self, family, community, Elders, and Creator / 15
2.1 Top and bottom of the Hand Drum gifted by my nation / 33
2.2 My first Secwépemc Hand Drum / 34
2.3 Understanding the Hand Drum as guide and metaphor for my inquiry / 35
3.1 Ned and Nancy Moiese, Georgina's grandparents / 51
3.2 Georgina in Grade 1 / 55
3.3 Cariboo Indian Student Residence crest / 68
4.1 Close look at an original Secwépemc basket, from all four angles / 90

SECWÉPEMC PRAYER

Kuwstec-kuc tqelt kukpi7 teskectec-kuc te tmicws
We thank you Creator for giving us this beautiful earth.

Yucwminte xwexweyt te stem ne7elye ne tmicw
Take care of everything on this earth.

*Yucwminte re qelmecw, tmesmescen, spipyuy̓e,
sewellkwe, ell re stsillens-kuc*
Take care of the people, the animals, the birds and our food.

Knucwente kuc es yegweyegwt.s-kuc
Help us be strong.

Kuwstec-kuc tqelt Kukpi7 te skectec kuc te xwexweyt te stem
We thank you Creator for giving us everything that we need.

•

Foreword

Have you wondered what Indigenous people mean when they speak about intergenerational learning or how Indigenous personal stories facilitate emotional or spiritual healing or how trauma is passed from one generation to the next? Have you wondered how Indigenous people can reclaim, revitalize, and reconcile Indigenous ways of knowing and being after experiencing decades of colonial harm to their rights, culture, and language? If so, I recommend that you read Georgina Martin's book, *Drumming Our Way Home*. We journey with her, Elder Jean William, and youth Colten Wycotte while they tell lived stories of being Secwépemc, and through a storied meaning-making process, the answers to these questions become real.

As an Indigenous educator and faculty member, I was fortunate to meet Georgina Martin when she began her doctoral studies in the Faculty of Education at the University of British Columbia. I also had the pleasure of supervising her doctoral research, which serves as the foundation for this book. During her graduate research, Georgina first started to use her Secwépemc Hand Drum and to sing the Women's Warrior song. As a beginner, she was sometimes hesitant, but she demonstrated commitment, persistence, and exceptional ability to learn until her voice and drumming actions became stronger. Georgina completed her doctoral research in the same way. Now, in this book, as an Indigenous scholar-author, she goes far beyond her research to create deeper understandings of Indigenous grandparents' and Elders' teachings and how they taught young people. Her voice, Hand Drumming, and ideas about individual and collective cultural identity, intergenerational learning and healing, and reconciliation are vibrant, far-reaching, and need to be shared widely.

After reading *Drumming Our Way Home*, I began to imagine that I was at an Indigenous cultural gathering where guests are invited to witness, to learn, sometimes to participate in the cultural work that is about to take place. Often, food is provided, drummers and singers will share various songs, a spokesperson will speak on behalf of the host family to facilitate the cultural work, other speakers will tell stories and share teachings, and there is a giveaway of gifts to show appreciation to the guests and those who assisted with the cultural work. Of course, much more happens in Indigenous cultural gatherings, depending on the community's protocols, culture, and purpose of the gathering.

I imagine that in this metaphorical gathering, each of the book's main speakers-storytellers has reached back into their historical memories to relive and reflect critically on some of their storied family and community experiences. Through this process, they have also gained new understandings based on heart-mind-body-spirit Indigenous storywork principles of respect, reverence, responsibility, reciprocity, holism, interrelatedness, and synergy. The concept of home as a place, family, and kinship with the land/environment and more-than-humans has shaped their cultural identity; as has the painful separation from home, family, and community through enforced attendance at Indian residential schools and an Indian hospital.

I imagine that I am asked to be a witness for this gathering. The role of the witness includes but is not limited to: watch/observe, listen carefully, remember what happened, and then share this knowledge with others. I begin this role by speaking directly to the storytellers and Indigenous guests:

> My dear ones – In my Stó:lō tradition, I raise my hands in thanks and respect to each storyteller for sharing your heartfelt and lived stories so that others can learn from your experiences. It takes courage to share the difficult moments of separation from family and community members and as young children, not knowing why. Yet, your stories show resilience and strength as you have kept Elders' and grandparents' teachings alive in your heart, mind, body, and spirit, waiting for the right time to live them once more. That time is now. I raise my hands in thanks and respect to each storyteller for continuing to live your Indigenous teachings and your willingness to share your learning journeys so that others are encouraged to learn and live their Indigenous ways of knowing and being.

Georgina Martin has created new story pathways for other Indigenous people who are wondering about ways to rekindle, reclaim, and revitalize Indigenous teachings to shape and strengthen one's Indigenous identity and to heal from the devasting effects of colonization. Her Indigenous storywork may guide the development of collective cultural identity too. However, these pathways need to become your own, through your stories, and your critical reflections and actions. Your powerful stories are needed now more than ever.

In my role as witness, I also speak to others who may be settlers, allies, educators, policy-makers, and the general public:

My dear ones – this book, *Drumming Our Way Home,* offers promise and possibility for concrete ways to address the Calls to Action of the Truth and Reconciliation Commission of Canada and the Canadian national legislation on the United Nations Declaration on the Rights of Indigenous Peoples. You have an opportunity to learn from Indigenous people whose stories exemplify the truth of and resistance to colonial impact. Take time to read this book carefully and slowly, think about how you can contribute to efforts of reconciliation, how you can facilitate improving relationships between Indigenous and non-Indigenous Peoples, and how you can support Indigenous Peoples' human and legal rights. Your stories of and actions for reconciliation are needed now more than ever.

Finally, in my role as witness I speak to everyone at this gathering. Sometimes the witness may share particular thoughts that were not spoken or considered:

My dear ones – I conclude my thoughts with a memory of one place mentioned in the book, which was the Coqualeetza Indian Hospital, situated on the unceded lands of the Stó:lō people in the Fraser Valley of British Columbia, where Georgina Martin was first separated from a key member of her family. Indian hospitals, like Indian residential schools, continued the harmful assimilative and separation processes for Indigenous people.

The memory I want to share is about the place of Coqualeetza, where the leadership and collective work of Stó:lō Elders and community members have reclaimed the land and facilities when the residential school and hospital closed. Today, the land of Coqualeetza is a place of cultural revitalization, education, health and social services, Stó:lō governance, and more. One of the Indigenous meanings of the traditional name of Qw'oqw'elith'a, from which Coqualeetza is an anglicized version, is a place of gathering and of cleansing. I was fortunate to learn from Stó:lō Elders who guided many to reclaim our stories, teachings, values, and culture and to tell our history from our lived experiences. Now, Indigenous communities are reclaiming lands and places for health and well-being that once were places of hurt and despair.

To conclude a cultural gathering, the host gives gifts that may be practical everyday items for the home, or traditional dried or canned foods, or handmade arts and crafts, and an item that has printed on it the date, place, and purpose of the gathering. These gifts are given in thanks and respect, for remembrance, and for practical daily living.

Drumming Our Way Home is both a valuable and practical giveaway that expresses thanks and respect to Indigenous grandparents and Elders for continuing to educate and guide others. The stories serve as a remembrance and pedagogy of past and present experiences that have shaped Indigenous individual and collective identity. This book offers hope and possibility for finding one's way to a meaningful concept of home and for contributing to concrete actions of reconciliation.

All My Relations,
Dr. Jo-ann Archibald Q'um Q'um Xiiem
Stó:lō and St'át'imc First Nations

Preface

The point of origin for my story is my birth: I was born in the Coqualeetza Indian Hospital. I was removed from my mother at birth because she was diagnosed with tuberculosis (TB) and therefore considered contagious. Indian hospitals were established to house Indigenous Peoples across Canada to control contamination. In my opinion, I was born into legislated interference.

My story emerges from my encounters, which I refer to as a lost "sense of belonging." Through discovery, I educated myself, to inform my community and the general public about what happens to an Indigenous person when they are invasively removed from critical aspects of their cultural identities. During my journey, I employed protocols and methods that support and protect the intense emotional work that accompanied my inquiry. These allowed me to engage safely and relationally in deep personal reflection.

I tell of my own lived experiences and share narratives that highlight the importance of knowing oneself. I blaze a path to assist other Indigenous Peoples to define their own identities. I establish how Indigenous Knowledge is anchored in our identities and connections to our cultural rootedness, inspired by the cultural teachings of grandparents and other prominent Elders. My autobiographical narrative captures the central tenets of intergenerational knowledge transmission, familial relationships, and land-based/culture-based learnings that are vital for safeguarding Secwépemc identities.

To anchor these connections, the Secwépemc Hand Drum epitomizes Indigenous Knowledge; it helps me remain balanced in upholding community protocols while honouring the Elders'/grandparents' teachings. Rather than succumb to external influences, which place Indigenous Peoples in a subjugated position, I uphold our places in research, academic institutions, and educating the general population. My story offers truth telling and a way forward to bring Indigenous Peoples back from the periphery of mainstream society.

Drumming Our Way Home

CHAPTER 1

Drumming as Metaphor

Whatever I am going to tell about my experience, as I go forward I am listening to the messages that I am getting from my surroundings because of my attachment to the land and the importance of the drum. I am listening to my intuition. It could be the beginning of the next part of my journey, I think it is.

- GEORGINA MARTIN

OPENING EPIGRAPH

My opening epigraph is a segment from a personal story I penned in 2009. This quote situates the complications I faced as I became attuned to who I am and to my reality. Going forward, I address the sense of exclusion, or what not "belonging" means, to ensure movement beyond disjointed identity formation. It is crucial for me to reclaim space and place while reasserting who I am as an Indigenous woman. The opening epigraph draws attention to the importance of listening, feeling, moving, and becoming as I journeyed forward.

This segment of my journey begins with receiving my first treasured Hand Drum. During one of my frequent stopovers to visit my long-time friend Lena Paul in Alkali Lake on August 2, 2002, she gifted me with my first Hand Drum.[1] I was not expecting to receive such a gift; the gifting and receiving of the drum is a significant honour. It is similar in stature to receiving an eagle feather. These traditional practices are widely recognized and highly revered. Our ancestral teachings tell us that gifts of this magnitude require time and preparation. There are many steps involved and Lena had prepared for this day for quite some time. The energy that goes into the making of the Hand Drum is very special because it is a very long process and tremendous care is applied as it moves through each and every step. Each person that handles the components of the Hand Drum does so with gentleness and respect. Only good energy goes into the creation and the creators feel a lot of pride in their work.

Accepting the Hand Drum compliments and parallels the value of the gift-giving. The person accepting the gift upholds the drum with care and responsibility. I accepted the drum knowing that I bore a huge responsibility to respect the drum and take care of it. I must keep the drum alive. This meant learning how to drum and sing with my new Hand Drum. My Hand Drum became a very sacred and prominent element in relearning my attachment to the land and rootedness in my identity. The Hand Drum's eminence kindly encircled me and became the foundation and strength that propelled me forward and anchored me while I delved into my beginnings. In a sense, when I chose to designate the Hand Drum as my pillar, the finished drum represented who I was when I took up the search for my identity in 2008 through my doctoral research. With the Hand Drum physically in hand as my metaphorical anchor, I began to unravel the state of my identity though personal inquiry and story. My early reflections begin with frank fullness and often stirred raw emotion, sometimes unexpectedly.

Only with Good Intentions

Given that I am peeling back the layers and exposing my identity from the standpoint of my lived experience, I must do so with gentleness and kindness toward both myself and Indigenous people in general. The Hand Drum became my spirit guide, ensuring my soul remained intact. I say this because at this juncture in life I still grapple with the lost sense of belonging that cumulated from a severe breakdown in my self-esteem. I link this loss to many life experiences that wounded my sense of self and prohibited me from my true Secwépemc identity. Because I am Secwépemc, and my origins emanate from my community of T'exelc, I felt that the Hand Drum showed me how to honour the inherent connections to my rootedness. The Hand Drum represents the life and the breath of identity that was instilled in me at a very young age.

The experiences that grievously shattered my sense of self includes my birth experience in the Coqualeetza Indian Hospital, the loss of culture and language in Indian day school, and residential school and its attendant and current reverberations known as intergenerational trauma. These are several phases that continue to torment my being, though I find that the detachment from my mother at birth carries the deepest emotional strain. I share these experiences with good intentions so I may help myself and others with similar experiences heal and journey forward. I work through a lens of resilience rather than one that would have me remain captive to deficit and dysfunction. Therefore, my scope and intent are to use my lived-experience stories as teaching stories for others with similar backgrounds to know they are not alone. It is crucial for people who have lived these experiences to garner the strength to listen to and retell their stories from a very real place. I say this because I am now an educator, and it is essential to lecture on these experiences in the classroom in ways that help students relate to these experiences. Finally, to the general public, I want to dispel the myth that Indigenous people can "just get over it." This is easier said than done.

Departure from My Mother's Womb
Beginning with the departure from my mother's womb, I experienced a massive disconnect from my spirit and soul. This disconnect mushroomed from the denial of human contact with my birth mother. My reality began when I was born in the government established Coqualeetza Indian Hospital. Consequently, my embodied experiences of disruption – dis/connection – are caught in the interplay between dichotomous responses to Indigenous identity lodged between validation and denial of my identity. I must first validate and assert my inherent identity as a Secwépemc woman,[2] then I approach the questions surrounding my identity, which corresponds with the 1876 Indian Act fabrication of Indigenous identities in Canada.

The grave influence of legislated interference on my being began at the government sanctioned sanatorium – the Coqualeetza Indian Hospital – which was established in 1941. This Indian hospital was located in Sardis, British Columbia (BC), which is 448 kilometres from my home community of T'exelc, in the interior of BC. T'exelc is in close proximity to the City of Williams Lake. Hence, the reality of my separation at birth weighed me down. While I was growing up in my community, I recall being told that my mother was quarantined with TB prior to and at the time of my birth. In later years, I learned that she was deemed to be contagious and placed in the Indian hospital to control the spread of TB. These federal government sanctioned Indian hospitals were set up to house "Indian" (as labelled by the Indian Act) people only. While researching the topic, the only printed source available was Laurie Meijer Drees's 2013 book *Healing Histories: Stories from Canada's Indian Hospitals*. I

Figure 1.1 Ned and Nancy Moiese, Georgina's grandparents. | Courtesy Georgina Martin

currently co-teach with Laurie at Vancouver Island University. It is exciting to work alongside her because she investigated Indian hospitals and spoke with many Indigenous people who shared their stories. She understood how the people who were placed in the Nanaimo Indian Hospital were gathered and subsequently treated during their stay. Most importantly, she confirmed how these hospitals exercised a specific agenda. It is true that the people were considered contagious. Before a cure emerged, the government authorities established a plan to isolate and contain the TB pandemic so the rest of the population would not be exposed to Indigenous people's deadly strain. As a result, TB and its attendant policies separated me from my birth mother. Thankfully, I was placed in the care of my maternal grandparents, Ned and Nancy Moiese (see Figure 1.1).

I chose to share my story and place this side by side with the stories Jean William and Colten Wycotte shared because of the importance of owning and sharing my story – all of our stories. Together, the three of us represent three generations: Elder, mid-life, and youth. Our uncovering of and learning about life stories helped us recognize and appreciate our Traditional Knowledge from a communal perspective. The stories highlighted our historical connections and our struggles to address the loss of our cultural identities. Knowing ourselves and becoming more attuned to our realities helps us to dispel the negative beliefs and stereotypes that were imposed on us by external forces. The dismissal of self-doubt, lack of confidence, and low self-esteem will help us reaffirm that we can succeed in many facets of life. From the outset of my research, I grappled with the inclusion of myself in the story, and I still do. I often wondered if my story was important and if I really had anything to teach through my experiences. Self-deprecation has made it difficult to accept the importance of unpacking components of my identity, stifled by the "so what and who cares" element of research. I needed to get to the heart of my own sense of loss in regard to who I am as a human being and as a Secwépemc person.

Situating Autobiography
After being grounded with the teachings of my grandparents and Elders in my community, receiving support from Stó:lō scholar Dr. Jo-ann Archibald, and connecting with my Hand Drum, I embarked on my personal transformation to unravel the layers of my inner being and rediscover who I am, really. The interest in exploring my embodied lived experiences led me toward autoethnography.

This autobiographical narrative takes place within a specific sociocultural and historical context. Part of this historical context is about my hometown of Williams Lake as described by Elizabeth Furniss. Furniss (1999, 4) described how the early white "discoverers celebrated their sense of the 'self-made man.'" This led to the demeaning stereotypes of Aboriginal peoples that denied them "their individuality, humanity, and integrity" (5). To counter this denial, our collective Secwépemc life histories purposefully validate and contextualize Secwépemc worldviews through the lens of the Secwépemc peoples. These historical experiences and stories that shaped our Secwépemc identities are not found in textbooks. By chronicling the lives of three Secwépemc people, we collectively recognize and reaffirm who we are as T'exelc people. The method by which D. Jean Clandinin and Michael F. Connelly (2000, 42) create "a new sense of meaning and significance in respect to the research topic" confirms the importance of preserving our identities, which we illustrate through our collaborative intergenerational experiences. My aims were to develop an understanding of how our Secwépemc identities were supported through Elder teachings and community connections. Through my relational and reflexive inquiry, I was compelled to focus on three themes: (a) to honour our Elders teachings and how they shaped our cultural identities, (b) to privilege the cultural identity of the Secwépemc people, and (c) to understand how stories define our cultural identities. The latter theme delves into how stories that were passed on from generation to generation shaped us, especially through the ways we connect with Elders. During this work, I realized the effects of dislocation, which Onowa McIvor (2012, 27) argued weakened our identity; more than severing our ties to family and community, separation "had hugely destructive psychological effects on many Indigenous people." It has also created generations of Indigenous people who have been left feeling empty and unfulfilled both culturally and spiritually.

I felt unfulfilled culturally and spiritually through my interactions within mainstream society and the public school system. As a means to contest Western worldviews, I positioned my research from within self and aligned my work with Shawn Wilson's paradigm. Wilson (2008, 15) proclaims that "Indigenous" is a process of reclamation, which means "relating to Indigenous people and peoples." I opted for "Indigenous" (rather than Aboriginal, First Nations, etc.) to align with Wilson's (16) claim that "Indigenous is inclusive of all first peoples – unique in our own cultures – but common in our experiences of colonialism and our understanding of the world." Both Indigenous and Secwépemc are my preferred descriptors in my study. Using these descriptors helped me refuse the external labels dictated by the federal government while contributing to a more autonomous sense of choosing how I want to be identified. I detest the label "Indian." I review the complexity of labelling in more depth in Chapter 2.

This book has two primary purposes: First, our stories can assist educators, policy-makers, and the general public to understand the effects of our embodied lived experiences as Indigenous people, especially residential school trauma and its intergenerational legacies. By understanding our lives, educators can more effectively intervene in cycles of marginalization and cultural alienation and policy-makers may come to a better understanding of how policy impacts Indigenous lives. Second, the book will help other Indigenous and non-Indigenous peoples of all backgrounds as they embark on their own identity journey. By grappling with my personal sense of loss, as well as my path to reclamation, others may acquire tools to work through their individual cultural narratives. Gregory Cajete (2000, 183) believes that "education is really about helping an individual find his or her face, which means finding out who they are, where you come from, and your unique character ... education should also help you find your heart." Teaching educators and others about how Indigenous Peoples are affected by trauma is the first step to creating change in the world.

Like many individuals and scholars who have journeyed back to their roots, my journey is personal and vital. Identity experiences vary; for me, it is a spiritual journey home, while for others it may be a continuing search for their community. In spite of the impact of false identities imposed on us through legislation, I believe a new day is coming when Indigenous Peoples will wholly and freely celebrate their cultures and identities, which were never extinguished. According to Furniss (1995, 43), "Shared kinship ties, language, and cultural values reinforced a sense of common identity among the Shuswap of the Cariboo."[3]

Indigenous cultural practices were almost demolished by the federal government's 1884 amendment to the Indian Act, which targeted culturally rooted identities by outlawing cultural practices. When potlatches and other ceremonial practices were banned, anyone caught practising, or perceived to be practising, any form of their culture or traditions were fined or jailed. This legislation was not repealed until 1951. Similarly, Indigenous languages were almost eradicated through residential school systems. These disruptions impeded the intergenerational transmission of cultural identities, resulting in a fragmented and misunderstood culture and modified cultural practices and spiritual teachings. But, despite the government's attempts to annihilate them, our Indigenous identities have not become stagnant, instead they have thrived.

In her examination of the 1987 *Regina v. Alphonse* court case, Andie Diane N. Palmer (1994) illustrates the assault on the practice of Secwépemc subsistence. As Palmer outlines, during the trial, Secwépemc witnesses made efforts to explain how the practice of subsistence is essential to the Secwépemc way of life. However, the Western legal system was hindered by its inability to comprehend the spirit of traditional subsistence practices. This inability to understand the witnesses' portrayal of subsistence hunting led to a denial of the defensibility of subsistence. The court decision dismissed, both literally and symbolically, the importance of hunting as a viable defence and the significance of the transfer of cultural knowledge practices.

Further variance in identities is attributed to the forced movement of Indigenous Peoples off their lands. I found that many Indigenous Peoples like me, who migrate to cities, may or may not know their cultures or have ways of practising culture. It is important for Indigenous Peoples to maintain linkages to their communal cultural identities. The absence of specific cultural practices in urban centres can be attributed to the diversity of the Indigenous Peoples who live in them. There is not one cultural practice that will apply to all Indigenous Peoples. We are all unique. The retention of culture in urban centres is stronger for Indigenous Peoples who are larger in numbers. To remain strong culturally, Indigenous Peoples will create space for themselves to gather and practice their culture. For those who are not culturally grounded, they may be drawn to more broadly delineated Indigenous events such as Pow Wows, National Aboriginal Day celebrations (June 21), or events similar to West Coast night (drumming and singing) at the Vancouver Aboriginal Friendship Centre. I feel that most Indigenous Peoples who have been connected to their culture and homeland have an inherent strength that moves them to satisfy their cultural void. On the other hand, there are people who do not know their cultural identities and who may never learn or enjoy them. Through my doctoral research, I affirmed that my grandparents, and their teachings, are the foundation of my cultural identity. I am grateful that they grounded me and kept me linked to embodied memories of my beginnings. The seeds planted from my connections to my nation and community combined with the consistent message my grandfather spoke, to "never forget who I am and where I come from," is what helped me retain my Secwépemc distinctiveness. I rely on these childhood memories of growing up with my grandparents to bring me back to my cultural beginnings.

While I planned and prepared to flourish in the Western academy, it was fundamental to bring my Indigeneity to the forefront. By bringing my Indigeneity into my academic work, I recognized and acknowledged the importance of Secwépemc culture. As part of this work, I reflect on how Secwépemc history could have been different if identity disruptions had not occurred. If our identities had not been decimated, the Secwépemc and other nations would have prospered culturally, politically, socially, and economically. I believe the importance of celebrating our Indigeneity cannot be underestimated if we are to ensure Indigenous Knowledges and worldviews are not compromised and deemed less important.

While the stories I offer in this book represent three examples of lived experience, many Indigenous Peoples have experienced interruptions and disruptions from family, culture, and homeland. Because of this interference, many people have developed defence mechanisms to protect themselves from trauma, which allows them to survive. One example of this is the way some Indigenous Peoples modify their behaviours and beliefs to fit into the present but without conforming or losing sight of themselves. By connecting with my story, I became more aware of the trauma that was transferred through the generations. I acknowledged my experiences and what I passed on to my family on various levels. My birth in an Indian hospital was my first experience of trauma, which was compounded by the absence of nurturing from my mother. On top of my Indian hospital birth, I accumulated residential school experiences from both me and my dad. Subsequently, I had experiences throughout my life that I now recognize contributed to learned behaviours. Due to my lived experiences, I developed defence mechanisms to ensure that no one got too close to me. I remained guarded to avoid emotional harm. But this had the unintended effect of closing off my emotions, which resulted in difficulties showing affection to my loved ones. As I moved through my research, I noticed that my defences played out in my writing, and I struggled with confidence and self-esteem. Thankfully, I have the capacity to return to the vital teachings of my grandparents to lean on them and to learn and heal. My journey to reclaim who I am begins with me and extends to my family, community, the Elders, and overall, the Creator, as shown in Figure 1.3. I intend to restore and restory Secwépemc values to their rightful place by teaching through our stories and embodied experiences.

Situating Education and Secwépemc Ways of Knowing

On my journey, I process how to honour my stories by acknowledging myself as a Secwépemc woman and ensure this connection is made in a meaningful way. Joyce Schneider (2008, 37) shares the complexity of process as she claims, "Many of us from Indigenous communities feel emotions of self-doubt and fear in today's academic environment. We feel that we must prove not only our research but also ourselves as Indigenous people, as legitimate." I believe I would have advanced academically and in my scholarship earlier if I did not experience self-doubt. I recall my science teacher when I was in Grade 8 encouraging me to pursue a university degree, and I blatantly refused because I dreaded stepping into an environment where I would feel unwelcome or where I might be forced to forsake who I am. I spent twelve years in a public education that situated me as an outsider peering up through the glass ceiling. I had my doubts that I could survive in a university environment, especially in 1973, when I graduated from high school. Not only was the closest university to Williams Lake at the time the University of British Columbia in Vancouver, a distance of 549 kilometres, but at the same time, I was not aware of any Indigenous scholars from my community or elsewhere that could inspire me. Nonetheless, the encouragement I received from my grandfather to get an education resonated. My grandfather always said it was important to get an education and bring it back to my people, and his words remained with me and kept me searching for more.

To truthfully self-actualize, I situate and connect with my community. Williams Lake is located in the interior of BC; I remained in its vicinity into my late twenties. Economic necessity brought me to Prince George, a two-and-a-half-hour drive north of Williams Lake. Although Prince George is

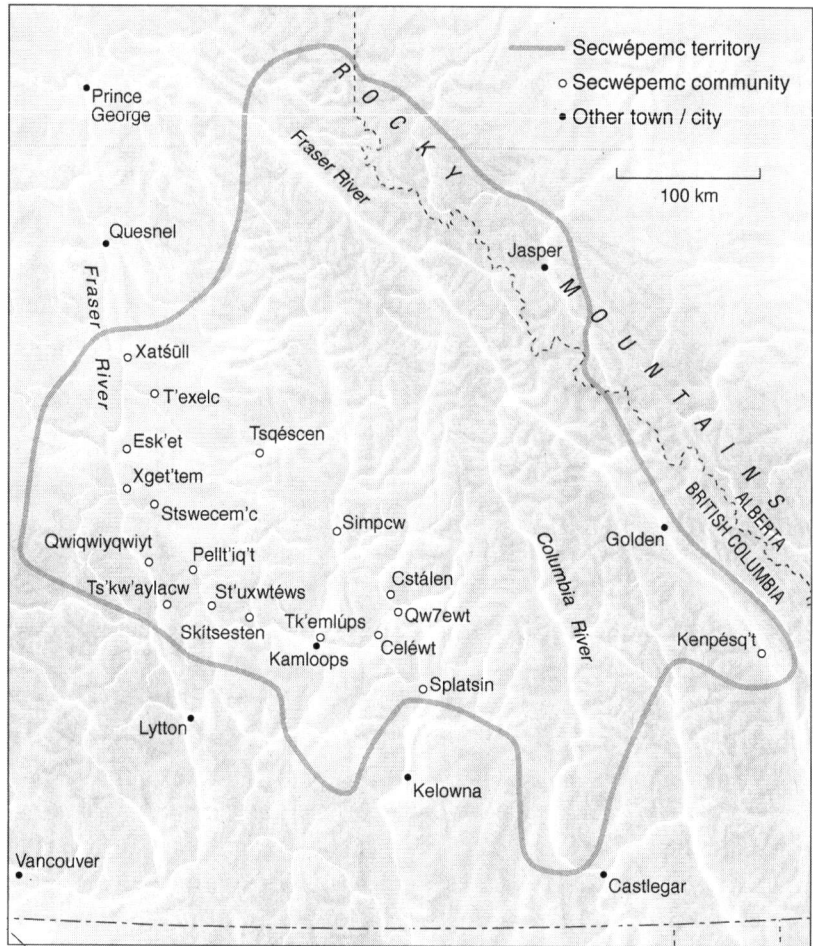

Figure 1.2 Map of Secwépemc Territory. | Original map courtesy Joanne Hammond, redrawn by Eric Leinberger

located in the middle of the province, it is considered the northern capital of BC. From 1984, I claimed Prince George as my home base.

I am from one of the seventeen Secwépemc communities in the central interior of BC,[4] and through marriage, I was previously an enrolled band member of Lake Babine Nation and am now a member of Williams Lake First Nation. My home village is historically known as Sugar Cane and the community reclaimed their Secwépemc name as T'exelc. Nancy Harriet Sandy (2011, 2) describes T'exelc as "a place where the salmon charge up the river," and suggests the name Sugar Cane "comes either from the sweet tall grass that grows there or from a story of sugar falling off a pack mule as a pack train travelled through." The language of the people is Secwepemctsín. Under the Indian Act, my community was also referred to as the Williams Lake Indian Band, though in January 2020, the name was legally changed to Williams Lake First Nation. The seventeen communities comprising the Secwépemc Nation are outlined in the map in Figure 1.2.

Sugar Cane is the place where I was raised by my grandparents, Ned and Nancy Moiese. I cherish very fond memories of my grandparents and my childhood with them. I credit them, and hold them both in high esteem, for being my primary caregivers and teachers of important Secwépemc values in my formative years. They cultivated the space for me to grow and develop a strong work ethic. My grandfather's teachings were especially powerful, and they keep me grounded; the Hand Drum generates the same connectedness. A significant teaching my grandfather bestowed on me is humility; the words he spoke that resonate within my conscience are "never to forget where you come from." I interpret these words to mean that wherever I go, I must always remember my beginnings and never imagine that I am better than anyone. Always remembering my community. Although this is an important teaching and it is highly revered among the Secwépemc people, it creates challenges in a postsecondary institution where we are expected to demonstrate domination and confidence. There is a great deal of effort required to balance our values and inner strength.

I absolutely agree with Indigenous scholars and leaders Verna Kirkness, Jo-ann Archibald, and Linda Tuhiwai Smith that positive Indigenous participation in education and research must be intensified to support the uptake of Indigenous Knowledge within academia. This could be achieved through the advancement of Indigenous pedagogies to create spaces for Indigenous scholarship. For Indigenous education to be effective, it must teach about our connections to land and culture. The land- and culture-based connections are integral in all areas of my research. I respect how my ties were never severed and I am attuned to certain aspects of my identity. My book contributes to educational success for Indigenous Peoples. I work toward connecting to place, culture, and identity to enhance Indigenous education. These connections help me and others journey home to Indigenous ways of knowing, and to knowing oneself.

Since entering the Doctor of Philosophy in Educational Studies at the University of British Columbia (UBC) in 2008, my primary academic goal was to contribute to and augment Indigenous Knowledge discourse for the advancement of Indigenous educational theory and praxis. My aim is to increase my capacity to influence educational and societal change, as well as to enhance my own effectiveness as an Indigenous scholar and educator. To achieve my goals, I must have a strong sense of who I am and how I represent Indigenous Knowledge from my communal perspective.

From the beginning of my educational journey, I was uneasy about how Indigenous students' life histories, which include their connections to family, culture, and communities, are absent from academia. In the Western education system, I was taught to think linearly rather than holistically. Linear outcomes are measured against preconceived guidelines and benchmarks, while holistic thinking is nonprescriptive. Jo-ann Archibald (2008) states that holism includes heart, mind, body, and spirit, whereas linear thinking is black and white, a right or wrong with minimal subjectivity or nuances. To remain holistic in my approach, I needed the autonomy to walk through the doors of the academy and keep myself intact with my family and community. Holism helps me to reflect on and reclaim who I am rather than deferring to a particular script, such as the imposed legislated Indian Act identity. Nonholistic thinking causes Indigenous Peoples to lose sight of who they are and discredits and devalues their being; self-doubt breeds the tacit acceptance of labels. I have the opportunity as one Secwépemc person to help myself and others believe in who we are and who we have become. I learned from my grandfather to remain connected to my roots. This is a cornerstone of my episteme.

In addition, my epistemological journey connects with my community's story. Drawing from my personal experiences, I explore threads of life histories along with two other Secwépemc relations who journey with me. My intergenerational study included Elder Jean William (Mumtre Nunxen xw te nek'wests'ut) and youth Colten Wycotte. Collectively, we are from the same community of T'exelc, where my study took place. We all preferred to use our real names rather than a pseudonym, although pseudonyms are used for relatives, acquaintances, and place names in stories. The anonymity of people and places adheres to cultural and communal protocols and also aligned with university ethics. This rigorous respect to the process helps me hold people and information in high esteem. The subject matter contained in this book has the potential to raise triggers that could elicit raw emotions. I have carefully considered this potential based on my own lived experiences. The goal is to impart critical teaching stories from a strength-based approach rather than reducing Indigenous people to a deficit. This approach requires a great amount of care. In addition, sacred place names associated with stories were not exposed to respect and maintain cultural integrity. It is not permissible to disclose certain family or community stories, aspects of the Secwépemc culture, and place names. My hope is to learn and teach from permissible stories and advance our collective worldviews.

By acknowledging our heritage, we find strength in our identities. Patricia Christine Rosborough (2012, 22) stated that "by placing Kwakwaka'wakw stories, language, and epistemology at the heart of my research, I engage in a process that strengthens my sense of identity and place in the world." I am looking for the same. I realize that language is a significant connecting factor to identity, but I do not focus solely on explicit indicators. Language connects us to the land. Identity is immense, and my examination of it stems from familial separation and the resultant distance from cultural identity. The telling and sharing of Secwépemc stories and life histories aligns with Rauna Kuokkanen's (2007) demand to open the academy's storehouse of knowledge and allow Indigenous philosophies and epistemes to be heard. The knowledge that I speak of is Secwépemc Knowledge, which is manifested in the community's collective ways of coming together through celebrations, stories, songs, language, and living off the land. Because "Indigenous storywork brings the heart, mind, body, and spirit together for quality education" (Archibald 2008, 153), my purpose is to bring the heart, mind, body, and spirit of Elder Jean, Colten, and myself together to produce Secwépemc pedagogical research into Secwépemc identities. To accomplish this, I must first make meaning of who I am and who I am becoming: I must return to my personal relational experience and locate myself as a Secwépemc person.

Speaking from a relational position is the best way to describe who I am because I embody the five spheres outlined in Figure 1.3 – self, family, community, Elders, and Creator.

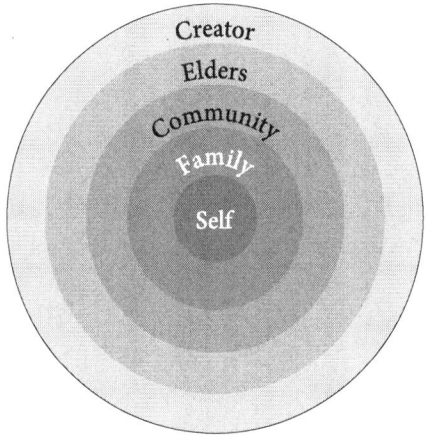

Figure 1.3 Relational sphere depicting the connections between self, family, community, Elders, and Creator. | Courtesy Georgina Martin

The relational aspects of the sphere are described by Eugene Richard Atleo (2004), who defines the physical and metaphysical as one; this concept is known as heshook-ish tsawalk in the Nuu-chah-nulth language, meaning the mind, body, and spirit are connected. Atleo's understanding is very similar to Archibald's concept of holism. My frame of reference operates in a circle; there is no beginning and no end, and all the parts are interconnected and equally important. I do not stand in isolation: embodiment represents my whole being. Embodiment allows me to reconnect with self through the reliving and retelling of my lived experiences, which is the integral framework that links me to heart, mind, body, and spirit. Cajete (1994, 74) elaborates that embodiment and holism is the way "Indians symbolically recognized their relationship to plants, animals, stones, trees, mountains, rivers, lakes, streams, and a host of other living entities." Holism is strengthened by "celebrating these natural relationships ... as living in a sea of relationships" (Cajete 1994, 74). Secwépemc Elders affirm that many Secwépemc people enjoy similar embodied cultural bonds with the natural world, and these cultural narratives are what shape us. The Secwépemc believed all living things, even rocks, fire, water, and other natural phenomena, to have souls because they were people during the mythological age (Favrholdt 2001, 14). The relational concepts and holistic nature of Indigenous ways of knowing stand in opposition to Western worldviews, which appear to conflict and are difficult to understand and articulate.

My Hand Drum Became My Guide

My lived-experience journey, with my drum in hand, led me back to important cultural values. The Hand Drum adheres with my cultural understanding and continued practice of carrying the Hand Drum with pride. Though I chose the Hand Drum to guide me and protect my work, I do not intend to suggest the Hand Drum should be the foundation for everyone's journey of self-discovery. For me, the Hand Drum represents my connection to my heart or lifeline, honesty, and integrity in my work, in who I am, and the overall importance of treating people with respect.

I discovered that while Western institutions retain colonial ideals, they can be places for Indigenous scholars to heal and reconnect, if they are given the opportunity. Through my participation in academia, I connected with my Hand Drum, and I began to sing public songs. Previously, I kept my Hand Drum safe and quiet. In 2008, while enrolled in Jo-ann Archibald's Indigenous Knowledges and Education course, I felt my Hand Drum beckon my spirit. During a seminar presentation, I presented my Hand Drum to the class and sang along with a taped recording of the Women's Warrior song, composed by Martina Pierre from Mount Currie. I was extremely nervous and mindful to honour the Hand Drum and the song by my actions. It felt quite uncomfortable, yet I knew I had to begin to honour my gift. Later, I continued to learn and practice drumming and singing with a group of women at the First Nations House of Learning at UBC. I was taught that there is no right or wrong way to drum and sing, what is important is the intent in your heart. I would say it took me an entire year of practising to learn how to comfortably lead the Women's Warrior song and I continue to practice a song from my home area. This is much the same as how I worked my way through academe, focusing on being right in my heart. The Hand Drum has deep personal meaning for me; I will inherently know if I am handling it correctly.

Dr. Archibald, Q'um Q'um Xiiem, is from the Stó:lō Nation, and she extended the opportunity for me and other students to connect with our spirits on a personal level. She offered us a class exercise in which we were to spend a few hours with nature (on the land) and engage in deep reflection while paying close attention to our surroundings. Each student chose the medium that suited them. I found a place of serenity alongside the Salmon Valley River, a twenty-minute drive north of the city of Prince George. During my walk by the river, I listened deeply to my surroundings and my spirit guide. Each time I recount this experience, I can immediately return to that time and place. As a result of those hours on the land, I found the courage to reach for my Hand Drum. Q'um Q'um Xiiem created sacred space for students to explore and value their gifts. Many students in her class made meaningful connections to places and spaces we may never have travelled to, in a metaphorical sense, if we had not taken part in her class. To this day, I return to the same spot by the Salmon Valley River when I need deep reflection. The area close to the river has changed, the trees I walked through in 2008 are no longer there, yet the feeling is the same. I feel a calmness that allows me to be in the moment with nature. I walk through the area while I admire nature and listen to the trees and birds. Before I depart, I drum and sing my one song to show my appreciation for the value the land has given me.

My research into Secwépemc identities aims to raise critical consciousness by affirming that Indigenous Peoples have strong cultural identities and explicit differences in terms of how we learn and view the world. Our learning is experiential and place-based. This work represents our stories: this will ensure that the value of community connections are sustained. If educators, policy-makers, and service providers recognize the delicate historical intricacies of Indigenous identity and well-being, they can use this knowledge to assist in revitalization. A holistic perspective governing policy, program content, and court decisions will be a welcome change. Indigenous Peoples will have the space to speak their truth on many levels. To speak and to be heard is to effect change. Shauna Lynn Bruno (2010, 41–2) speaks to "making a societal contribution, even in a small way (and that is all that is needed to make a difference). If it is only my children that I teach, then hopefully I have reached their generations to come." Her resolve gave me comfort as I struggled and strained to position my study within its wider academic context.

The way future generations are taught is vital because many Indigenous Peoples are stricken with intergenerational posttraumatic stress, explains Eduardo Duran (2006). I learned that, through institutional experiences imposed through Indian hospital and residential school placements, I am emotionally stricken. I carry the residual or cell memories that evolved from my mom's history at the Indian hospital and my dad's exposure to residential school. I am still mired in the grip of resultant traumas, which caused me to pass on several embodied experiences to my children and their children. Duran (2006, 16), using the concepts of "intergenerational trauma, historical trauma, and the Native American concept of soul wound," contends that when trauma is passed on through generations it is cumulative, so unresolved trauma becomes more severe for each person it passes through. Duran explains that when the experiences are not dealt with in previous generations, they then have to be dealt with in subsequent generations. My hope is that sharing parts of my story will contribute to the healing of future generations, in both my family and in others. I hear that it will take seven generations for families to escape the grip of intergenerational or multigenerational trauma.

I realize that I am not alone on this journey; many Indigenous scholars (Bruno 2010; Cardinal 2010; Lessard 2010; Young 2003) have spoken about a process of restorying who they are. Part of me affirming and regaining my presence is understanding the importance of cultural identity for Indigenous Peoples and communities. Kathryn A. Michel (2012, 23) acknowledges the urgency of reclaiming our cultural identities; she iterates that in order to confront the "colonizing forces of assimilation, we need to take back our right to our own histories." The fallacy of a legislated identity dictated by the Indian Act triggered for me the holistic importance of possessing my Secwépemc identity and culture through self-actualizing and reclaiming. I do remain constricted by the federal government label of being "Indian" in accordance with Indian Act definitions because our nations did not retain the autonomy to decide who we are as a people. It is infuriating to be legally labelled under a foreign Indian Act that fabricates our identity and adds confusion. To refute this legislated identity, I must honour and privilege my Secwépemc identity first and foremost. To do so, I locate myself within, and in relation to, my Secwépemc culture. To move forward, it is absolutely critical for me and other Indigenous Peoples to eradicate the tensions between Eurocentric and Indigenous worldviews and restore our epistemological and ontological integrity. Integrity is mandatory given that Indigenous people are so diverse. No one can create any kind of categorization or typology of Indigenous epistemology and ontology because many themes overlap and are interconnected, as scholars Atleo (2004) and Cajete (1994) have affirmed. I personally recognize that we can be connected to our homelands in a semi-spiritual or spiritual way. By this I mean that we may have experienced attachment to the land in our formative years and physically moved away from our homeland, but we remain connected in our own way. For some Indigenous Peoples, who may not know their homeland or had any communal ties, there is a missing link and they may go in search of their roots to help them feel whole. Hawaiian scholar Manulani Aluli-Meyer situates our relationships with our environments as spiritual as well. She believes "ontology is the philosophy of essence – who you are, who are your people, where are you from, what difference does that make to you? That's ontology" (2001, 195). This is what I hope to answer.

Holistic ontology refers to the clear connection between individual, community, land, and the universe. Conversely, the nature of Western knowledge is to objectify reality, and in this sense, it challenges Indigenous epistemes in which the premise of reality is focused on an inward journey. My research was premised on my and my participants' inward journeys. Unearthing our epistemes will reverse the manner in which "the epistemology of our past has been compartmentalized into scattered pieces and removed from our lives" (Ignace 2008, 53). My "stories lived and told" (Clandinin and Connelly 2000, 20) link me to the embodied experience of being Secwépemc; as I explained in the preceding sections, this embodiment includes my Hand Drum. The Hand Drum reverberates between honouring and exemplifying my return to my beginnings and connectedness to my people. I am on a journey home in many ways; to reconnect to who I am and who I am still becoming.

Indigenous Knowledge from the Heart

I further valued Indigenous Knowledge from the heart when I attended the Building Peaceful Communities Summer Institute at the University of Alberta in July 2009. There, I experienced Indigenous Knowledge in a sharing circle led by Sean Lessard, a First Nations scholar, and Florence Glanfield, a Métis scholar. Sharing circles are common practice for Indigenous Peoples and communities across Canada; each community adheres to an array of cultural protocols specific to their nation based on important teachings and traditions. I have participated in several sharing circles for healing purposes but rarely in an academic institutional setting. In this particular setting at the Peace Institute, the sharing circle signified a place of respect. Each person was given an opportunity to share or not share, depending on how they felt. A physical object was passed around, and only the person who held the object would share whatever they needed to without questions or interruptions.

During the sharing circle, which included participants and instructors, two profound events occurred for me. One was when Sean Lessard shared words he received from an Enoch Elder, Bob Cardinal: "The longest journey we will ever make is from our head to our heart." I was really touched by these words because they resonated with my emotional losses and, specifically, my inability to show affection as a result of being removed from my mother at birth; I know how important heart work is. The message spoke to me because I am on a personal journey to move from my head to my heart with my Hand Drum, which will bring me where I need to be. Listening to the heart is crucial to celebrating Indigenous Knowledge. I am learning to listen more intently to the values that emanate from the land and the ancestors. This brings balance; as a human being I understand the importance of the heart as the physical body's life force and, equally important, as an Indigenous person I understand that listening to the heart is part of my Indigenous Knowledge. I continued to learn how to Hand Drum and allow the drum's spirit to guide me through academia and beyond.

The second event that happened at the Peace Institute is when I shared in the circle about my grandparents. Prior to attending the course, I was asked to bring an artifact that was meaningful to me, and I brought the photo of my grandparents shown in Figure 1.1. I acknowledged my grandparents as my trusted guides who bequeathed their support to me for the important road ahead. As I spoke about them, a magical happening took place. I mentioned in the circle that I was moving forward, believing that I am doing the right thing and hoping that my grandparents would approve. It was a dark overcast day and rain was expected at any moment. As I was speaking, an instructor on the opposite side of the room said the sun shone directly on me from behind. She believed that it was my grandparents giving me their blessing; I, too, believe this was the case. Standing beside the Hand Drum are my ancestors, particularly my grandparents, from whom I seek and receive guidance, I feel their presence as I embrace Indigenous Knowledge. My spiritual connections are examples of how I diverge from Western thought and join with my Secwépemc ontology.

My Awakening with Renewed Understanding of Indigenous Knowledge
Indigenous Knowledge is a vital system that respects the different ways of being of Indigenous Peoples and responds to their ways of knowing. The acknowledgment and sacredness of stories and the honouring of their truth requires a justifiable framework conducive to Indigenous Knowledge. My study depicts my own awakening and connection to Indigenous Knowledge. I regard Indigenous Knowledge as validation and strength; it gives me the opportunity and courage to reflect on and articulate my Indigenous values, beliefs, and ideas.

To inspire my reflection, I recall these questions posed by Linda Tuhiwai Smith (2010) in her keynote address at Trent University's tenth anniversary celebration of their Indigenous Studies PhD Program:

1. What have we learned about ourselves?
2. How do we know what we know?
3. How does Indigenous Knowledge help us to become who we are?

According to these epistemological questions presented by Smith, we must look inward to find the answers. She explained "inward" to mean going deep within oneself to the depth of the soul, to be in tune with one's being. This is the splendour of Indigenous Knowledge; there is no single directive on how to apply it, nor is there a standard definition to describe it. Rather, Indigenous Knowledge varies and its defining principles rest upon the Indigenous person and their territory. Indigenous Knowledge is expressed within each nation according to their distinct culture; it is an essential part of the groups' identity. To do this work, it is important to remain connected to your community physically and spiritually. Smith further asserts that lessons learned from Indigenous Knowledge may not be immediate. Some people may go along in life and suddenly a lesson will appear. For others, lessons may not be noticed for quite some time, if at all. Elder Jean William, a participant in my study, showed me an example of Indigenous Knowledge transmission. At the beginning of the research process, during preliminary discussions about identities and what it means for the community, Elder Jean made an observation that I did not quite understand at the time. She said, "You are not Secwépemc unless you return to the land" (personal communication, February 10, 2011). Secwepemcúl'ecw is further explained to show how the Secwépemc are connected to the land: [*Secwep*] means unfolding/spreading out and coming home; [*emc*] is people of; [*úlecw*] is the land of, place of, territory. I wondered what this lesson meant and how to interpret it. As I progressed through my research, I felt the connection to my homeland become increasing important for me personally and it finally dawned on me recently that the important connection between place and identities for Secwépemc people is how people return to their land of origin. This lesson was reaffirmed by observing my eldest son and daughter in the ways they return to the land. My son hunts for moose and deer in the Secwépemc territory and my daughter actively engages in traditional food gathering and preserving on the land where she lives; this affirms that they are rooted through the cultural teachings they acquired from their grandparents.

Smith also reiterates that Indigenous Knowledge is not linear or prescriptive; rather, understanding Indigenous Knowledge becomes apparent over time. The same principle is enshrined in Archibald's *Indigenous Storywork: Educating the Heart, Mind, Body, and Spirit* (2008). Both Smith and Archibald developed striking examples of how Indigenous Knowledge is distinct from Western knowledge systems that rely on universal "objective" truths, categories and hierarchies that partition knowledge. Indigenous Knowledge is not partitioned, slotted into categories, or shaped into a mould; it is fluid. It is important for Indigenous Peoples to think, feel, and act based on their own moral, ethical, and cultural teachings. For me to do so, I must return to my childhood memories of my relationship with my grandparents.

To realize my cultural bonds, I was drawn to Clandinin and Connelly's (2000, 43) reference to narrative inquiry as the "embodiment of lived stories" because my embodiment extends to my community and Secwépemc people culturally. I am appreciative that I can legitimately convey my cultural strength through the memories of my grandparents. Likewise, Cajete (1994, 34) characterizes connectedness within an Indigenous context in terms of how "Indigenous groups used ritual, myth, customs, and life experience to integrate both the process and content of learning into the fabric of their social organization. This promoted wholeness in the individual, family, and community." Learning from our grandparents and Elders is a key component of social organization.

Historically, our values were attacked by external forces that disrupted Secwépemc traditions, knowledge, lifestyle, organizational systems, and especially identities, causing them to fracture, leaving in their wake a displaced sense of individual and collective identities. My exploration is an example of the struggles faced by a collection of Secwépemc people. My research helps me understand how the loss of identities affected my ability to acknowledge and validate my cultural beginnings. Understanding identity losses is essential to help me and other Indigenous Peoples move forward, to self-actualize, and to become self-empowered and contribute to the well-being of our families and communities.

To guide me further, I relied on Verna J. Kirkness and Ray Barnhardt's (1991) pivotal article about Indigenous education, "First Nations and Higher Education: The four Rs – Respect, Relevance, Reciprocity, Responsibility." I aligned the moral and ethical foundation of my Secwépemc identity study with these four Rs. Kirkness and Barnhardt (1991, 2) addressed how, from the institution's perspective, the problem of low Indigenous student numbers has been typically defined in terms of "low achievement," "high attrition," "poor retention," "weak persistence," but from the students' perspective, there is a need for a higher educational system "that *respects* them for who they are, that is *relevant* to their view of the world, that offers *reciprocity* in their relationships with others, and that helps them exercise *responsibility* over their own lives" (1991, 9, italics in original). Like many Indigenous scholars, my research begins with the utilization of Kirkness and Barnhardt's four R principles of Indigenous education in an Indigenous research context because they are critically important and relevant for community engagement. Accordingly, my application of storytelling and narrative is guided by Kirkness and Barnhardt's four Rs. In the world of academia, they help me to create space for *my* mode of being.

The four R principles complement cultural protocols that are essential when conducting research with and for Indigenous Peoples. I am an Indigenous researcher who returned to my home community. Hence, I engaged with my community in ways that tendered respect, relevance, reciprocity, and responsibility as baseline considerations for engagement between the Indigenous researcher and the Indigenous community. For instance, all who were involved respected each other and the mandate of the project; relevancy materialized in terms of what I could offer the community for future development based on the community's wants and needs; reciprocal relationships occurred through back-and-forth information sharing; and we all worked responsibly by respecting ethical boundaries while adhering to academic and communal accountability. To translate the four Rs into a research relationship meant honouring Traditional Knowledge and cultural values, capturing the essence of Indigenous viewpoints, being responsive in giving back, and listening and engaging with the community. Therefore, the four R principles were incorporated into my methodology.

Accomplished Indigenous theorists who honour Traditional Knowledge and cultural values include Jo-ann Archibald (1997, 2008), Eugene Richard Atleo (2004), Marie Battiste (2000), Gregory Cajete (1994, 2000), Graham Hingangaroa Smith (1997), and Linda Tuhiwai Smith (1999), to name a few. Each of these theorists reflects on their particular cultural beliefs, traditional practices, and relationships with the environment and with one another as part of their knowledge-seeking and -making process. Given that Indigenous worldviews are rooted within each nation's culture, the understanding of Indigenous Knowledge is rooted within the shared philosophies, values, and traditions of the people. The above theorists emphasize research ethics and protocols conducive to conducting research within Indigenous communities holistically and spiritually. To adhere to cultural protocols, I learned how to rely on my Hand Drum to support me in my work and to help me think clearly about my contributions to education, community, and Indigenous Knowledge. Indigenous Knowledge has created a feeling of legitimacy for me, although it is not highly accepted in academic spaces – most likely because it is not fully appreciated or understood. Kathleen Absolon (2011, 58) explains how Indigenous Knowledge works for Indigenous scholars: "The awareness and methodologies we have about ourselves in relation to Creation is integrated into our methodologies as we locate and story ourselves into our search processes. Our worldview/roots are informed by our ancestral lineage, our personal and political history, our cultural makeup, our nations and the sacred laws that govern our care and occupation of Mother Earth." Therefore, Indigenous scholars and researchers often do not separate themselves from their research; rather, they are a part of the research, and many connect with a culturally embedded framework to represent Indigenous Knowledge – mine is the Hand Drum. This method/arrangement may be very difficult for non-Indigenous scholars to understand. However, rather than seeing this as a reflection on the legitimacy of Indigenous Knowledge research methods, this should be understood as a struggle to integrate Indigenous Knowledge into the mainstream Western scholarly tradition.

Following the path of Indigenous scholars (Absolon 2011; Anderson 2011; Bruno 2010; Rosborough 2012; Steinhauer 2001; Young, 2003), I understand Indigenous Knowledge to be essential for my research involvement with Secwépemc identities. For instance, Absolon (2011, 55) explains how "the past, present and future intersect, and much of our research is about searching for truth, freedom, emancipation and ultimately finding our way home." This is my story to find my way home; before I get there, I must acknowledge the struggles Indigenous Peoples like me face to reclaim and celebrate our identities. It is often a heart-wrenching experience. The passion to retain and reclaim identities is what drives me as I express my own personal dislocation from my Secwépemc identity. It was important for my research that I explore how Secwépemc cultural ancestries mitigate the cultural interface between Indigenous and Western ways of knowing, and it helped me adopt a Secwépemc pedagogy. The cultural interface was introduced by Martin Nakata (2007) as a crucial tool for reconciling dual knowledge systems. He proposes that Indigenous Peoples proceed with care because, by being educated in a Western system, they run the risk of accepting a subjugated position; if this were to happen, our role in the education system would be counterproductive. The connection to my beginnings is represented by my Hand Drum. These tools are my physical, spiritual, and metaphorical guides.[5] These are what aided me to navigate between Indigenous and Western worldviews, and ultimately, allowed me to find ways to interact with both my community and the education system.

According to Absolon, many Indigenous researchers rely on their personal life-teachings and experiences in their work. The goal of a personal story is "to learn more about our Indigenous self, history, worldview [and] culture" (2011, 70) to balance the interface between Indigenous and Western worldviews. The best outcome is for Indigenous Peoples to enjoy autonomy legally, politically, and socially.

The significance of Indigenous Knowledge is supported in Archibald's (2008, 42) statement that "Aboriginal people have said that to understand ourselves and our situation today, we must know where we come from and know what has influenced us." Indigenous Knowledge is the foundation of what I need to support my understanding of being Secwépemc as it relates to a sense of belonging. I foster my sense of belonging through the Hand Drum, which returns me to my Secwépemc beginnings. Most importantly, the Hand Drum and drumming nurtured my spirit during my inquiry. With it, I always felt safe and balanced.

CHAPTER 2

The Drum Reverberates against the Intergenerational Aspects of Colonialism

The disease/dis-ease associated with colonial trauma has severed the teachings in my life today as an adult. The onus is now on me to continue learning and living these teachings, taking responsibility to share with others who are on a similar healing journey.

- RUPERT RICHARDSON 2012, 16

Exploring What Identities Represent

In my decision to dissect and decipher what identities mean, I privilege my origins in a proactive effort to dismember the Indian Act. The Indian Act frames Indigenous people under a false colonial identity. Another label that has come to constitute us is that of "Aboriginal," defined and written into the Canadian Constitution Act of 1982. I agree with Lisa Monchalin (2016), who argues that these false labels are a mechanism of colonization that maintains a powerful assault on Indigenous Peoples. Therefore, I examine my exploration of identities through the disruptive experiences I had that cumulated with feelings of a loss of self and a broken view of the world. For quite some time, I felt a missing link between my formative development and who I have become. I was not entirely sure what caused this feeling, but I was held down by it. I was raised by my maternal grandparents so I felt attached to them and my homeland. I found that my embodied experience is similar to that of an adoptee; though not in every way; for example, I grew up with my family and community and so I have a good sense of my roots. While I grew up in a caring and supportive environment, there was, and continues to be, a sense of injury to who I am and where I belong. I recognize that I am not alone, there are many Indigenous Peoples who share my experience. At the crux of my discovery are the traumatic experiences that disrupted Indigenous identities for well over two hundred years. Undergoing an exploration of self is a heart process. I travelled to the depth of my soul to unravel my lived experiences and learn from them. By positioning my story at the forefront of my inquiry, I knew that I must stress the teachings of my grandparents to retain respect and ensure that I bring honour to my family and my community. The moral foundation of this work is vital. This book encompasses a path of self-actualization, reclamation, and renewal.

Through self-actualization, I fixated on understanding the traumatic experiences that disrupted Indigenous identities for many years. The Indian Act led the assault that included the programs of Indian hospitals and residential schools. Recently added to these assailants are Indian day schools on-reserve. The Indian day school program contributed to the loss of culture and language by refusing to teach these languages and cultures or even permit them to be practised. English was taught instead of Secwepemctsín, which led to the loss of important identity connections in our formative years and contributed to our lack of agency to learn about and celebrate our identities. I continue to experience the legislated dictation of Indian Act identity along with the intergenerational effects of residential school and the resultant losses of being birthed in an Indian hospital. I am also continually faced with the inability to show affection to my loved ones, to speak my language, and to practice our traditions. The sharing and exploring of my own experience helps to mend the sense of injustice and supports self-transformation. I make an important contribution by affirming Indigenous identities and finding a voice for myself and for others.

I also articulate my contextual Secwépemc approach, my praxis. The process is transformative because I reclaim ownership of my cultural identity by returning to my homeland, transforming and reconnecting with my Secwépemc beginnings. My ideas are transdisciplinary because there are no boundaries when it comes to learning and acknowledging identities; identity surfaces for Indigenous Peoples in many places. This approach contributes to the growing demand that Indigenous Knowledges and methodologies be heard and to the self-empowerment of the Secwépemc and other Indigenous Peoples.

An Indigenous praxis begins with an acknowledgment of where one comes from and includes the recognition of one's historical, political, and social location. As Manulani Aluli-Meyer (2008) said, "True intelligence is self-knowledge."

I am an Indigenous scholar and researcher, therefore, I follow these principles: first, by learning to respect who I am and, second, by conducting research that is relevant for the community. Throughout, I aim to enact reciprocal consideration for the community's values about Secwépemc identities.

As my journey began, I struggled with the notion of piecing together cultural identities as a contribution to T'exelc in a way that would also fulfill my academic program. Accordingly, Rosborough (2012, 39) said, "Put into action what it means to be Indigenous." She found her Indigeneity by learning what it meant to be Kwakwaka'wakw; for me, my Indigeneity connects me to what it means to be Secwépemc.

At the beginning of my journey, during Dr. Archibald's course, my Hand Drum beckoned me. The first step to reclamation was learning to use my Hand Drum. I returned to affirming and continuing to connect with my cultural beginnings. I began by expanding my knowledge about the qualities of my Hand Drum. I took up the responsibility to seriously learn about and pass on the teachings associated with the Hand Drum while continuing to develop a response to the "disease" that is colonial trauma (richardson 2012). I knew that story and embodied experiences were the strongholds for my inquiry; the Hand Drum contains the embodiment of Indigenous Knowledge, which espouses Secwépemc identities. McIvor (2010, 138) refers to her worldview as a "cultural and spiritual way, with my ancestors walking beside me." I am like-minded in my approach. I walked with Elder Jean and Colten and beside my ancestors to find my spiritual way.

Identity Stories Emerge

While I envisioned how to roll out the three sets of embodied stories to come, I was reminded of the precision needed to prepare the animal hides for making the drum, as well as other items. While Hand Drums can be made from a variety of hides, such as elk, the original Secwépemc Hand Drum is made from deer or moose hide. Before the animal's life is taken, the hunter pays reverence and respect to the animal for giving their life for food and their hide. Several precautions are taken to ensure the high quality of the finished product, such as acquiring the hide from the deer or moose at the right time of the year. This ensures that the hide retains its strength and remains intact throughout the process and into longevity. The hide is scraped and all of the animal's hair is removed and then the hide is softened; this is a very long process. The drum maker ensures the consistency of the hide so the skin will secure tightly over the frame. When the raw hide is ready, each piece is measured to fit the wooden frame of the drum. The hide is stretched over the frame, keeping it taut. While it must stay taut, extreme care must be taken to ensure the tightness is not excessive; if it is, the hide will crack or rip when it dries. Caution is needed to avoid making the face of the Hand Drum too tight or too loose. The surface consistency will ensure that the drum has longevity, and it will withstand the elements. Because the animal's spirit remains with the Hand Drum, the Hand Drum is always alive. The drum is not an object; it lives and breathes. This is why we never refer to the drum as a thing; it is a being.

Thinking about the preparation of the hide for drums brings me back to my childhood and memories of my grandmother tanning hides. I clearly remember her placing the hides in the creek, holding them in place with rocks for a number of days while the swift water removed the hair. As a young child, I recall that taking about a month. When it was removed from the creek, the hide would then be soaked with the animal's brains in a large aluminum bathtub to soften it. Then the hide would be draped over a small pole with a point at the top to hold the hide and prevent it from slipping. Then it would be scraped to remove any remaining hair. After this phase, my grandmother, Nancy, would anchor the hide to a large, square wooden frame where it was delicately kneaded with a blunt tool to soften it in preparation for curing. The wooden frame had to hold the hide with a certain tautness during this phase. Finally, the hide would be dried and smoked, after which it could be used for making various products. The delicate care given to the hides is the same that is required in the collection and release of personal stories and lived experiences. As one takes care in handling hides, so too must I prepare myself for taking up and sharing the participants' stories in a way that is inherently respectful and reflexive. With careful thought and consideration, I brought together Indigenous storywork and narrative inquiry. I did not intend to create a dichotomy between Indigenous storywork, which I used for the participants, and narrative inquiry, which I used for myself. It was not my intention to suggest that Indigenous storywork cannot do the work of narrative inquiry. Instead, by weaving together the tenets of both Indigenous storywork and narrative inquiry, I was able to apply key aspects from each and incorporate them into a context that worked best for my story sharing. For example, I applied narrative inquiry when personally connecting with my story at a deep emotional level by moving inward and outward. In similar fashion, Indigenous storywork connects with the sharing of lived stories that are traditional and cultural.

To build on Indigenous storywork in the sharing of participant stories, I started where Archibald left off. Archibald (2008, 112) states, "Many First

Nations storytellers use their personal life experiences as teaching stories in a manner similar to how they use traditional stories. These storytellers help to carry on the oral tradition's obligation of educational reciprocity." This approach is framed as a giveaway; Archibald lays these teachings out to be taken up in ways that respect the principles of Indigenous storywork while offering Indigenous storywork as a methodology to use in different research contexts for different purposes.

In the story chapters, I share the personal stories of my lived experience to sort through my misgivings about my identities, while in sharing her personal life experiences as teaching stories and offering traditional practices for community members who are willing listeners and learners, Elder Jean's story is an example of a giveaway. Colten's story follows as a composition of learning stories that track how he relates to identities in his youth. In presenting Jean's and Colten's stories, I did not decode or analyze them; rather, I tell and share their stories as articulated through their voices. Through the projection of their voices, I unravel the significance or revolutionary meaning of their stories. Kimberly M. Blaeser (1999, 54) argues that this style of storytelling helps "weave people into the very fabric of their societies." Both Jean and Colten are very connected to their beginnings and they are in the best position to release and express the meaning of their experiences.

I reiterate how my birth in an Indian hospital distorted my sense of identity. Sadly, other than knowing I was born in the Coqualeetza Indian Hospital, I have not yet gathered the courage to examine the legacy of Indian hospitals much further. However, on September 24, 2012, while observing a class at the Chilliwack campus of the University of the Fraser Valley, I did learn that the TB hospital where I was born had been a residential school first.

Interestingly, my innate sense of what I term as a lost sense of belonging is confusing because I know without a doubt that I was cared for, nurtured, and trained by my grandparents. In my quest to understand this experience, I recall reading an article about an adopted person's experience. It was about feelings of abandonment and how it felt to have the nurturing ties between them and their mother severed. The story made sense to me because my situation was very similar. My ties with my mother were cut like the umbilical cord at birth simply due to my mother's medical condition. She was quarantined in the Coqualeetza Indian Hospital with TB at the time of my birth. To this day, I have not uncovered when my mother became a resident of the Indian hospital, nor do I know when she was released. I cannot answer if I was with her there for the full term of my utero development either. There are so many unanswered questions, and they are likely to remain unknown.

I cannot deny that, throughout my life, this experience affected me emotionally and spiritually. These feelings of loss messed with my spirit and reached into the depth of my soul. To this day, I have moments where I yearn to experience a close mother and daughter relationship. There are many times when I long for my mom, especially around celebrations like Mother's Day or when I need advice about life.

As I began to piece together identities and reflect on our absence in the history of Williams Lake, I enlisted the experiences of two Secwépemc community members to consider how our Secwépemc life histories can help change the historical landscape within the area. For me personally, my identities project was heart wrenching because it pushed me to places I rarely ventured into at the time. Over the years, I became conditioned to avoid thinking about deeply painful and traumatic experiences. To begin my journey, the Hand Drum consistently and constantly reminded me that my work is surrounded with the same care, protocols, and attributes as the Hand Drum itself. In essence, the Hand Drum became my strength and my moral and ethical guide.

The avoidance and fear I felt was not unusual, according to Aluli-Meyer (2008), who speaks about how a set of ideas can bring you back to remembering. She explains that the remembering extends from our Indigenous epistemology and brings us into a world of awakening. This is the process I undertook. I acquired my episteme from my grandparents and through my research journey, I was awakened to my inheritance of Secwépemc Knowledge. I connected to Aluli-Meyer's (2008, 224) concept that "genuine knowledge must be experienced directly" because the direct experience helps to organize the research mind. I spent considerable reflexive time carefully becoming part of the research, beginning with situating my connection to my grandparents and the Hand Drum. It is a continuous enterprise to become an "architect of meaning" (224) in order to establish my road map. While I moved along to address the stories, I understood how "knowledge that endures is spirit driven" (218). I combined and embraced the spirit, presence, and essence of my grandparents, Hand Drum, ancestors, Creator, Indigenous storywork, participants, and homeland in my work. My hope is to rekindle this spirit and keep it alive.

The Hand Drum as Metaphor

Kim Anderson (2000, 143) notes that "music, singing and drumming are integral to Native cultures." I recognize that, as with many Indigenous Nations, the songs, dances, stories, and ceremonies of the Secwépemc are important to our daily lives. The ceremonies are vital for maintaining the values, beliefs, and teachings of the Secwépemc regarding care of the land, animals, and the people. The Hand Drum represents the Secwépemc connection to the land and reminds the people of their responsibilities to both land and community. A practised example of the Hand Drum's reverence with the land is captured by the Secwépemc song and prayer that precedes the harvesting of food, medicines, and other materials from the land. Secwépemc people make an offering to thank the Creator and the spirits for what is taken, especially the life of the animals and anything else that is sacrificed. The Secwépemc believe that all inanimate objects have spirits that must be respected. Fellow T'exelc community member Kristy Palmantier tells of her experiences with Hand Drumming while growing up in the community, saying:

> My grandmother Celestine and my mom Elizabeth were both Hand Drummers. In fact, that's what I grew up with them singing all the time in the evenings, especially in the winter time. I used to have to dance for candy! My grandmother Celestine used to sing whenever she got the chance, in the parades, and at the stampede. I and Doreen always had to get dressed up in buckskin and dance while she drummed and sang. I remember we danced for Princess Margaret way back when she came to town ... sometime in the '60s. She and Ol' George Myers from Stone used to sing together at home and at stampede time too. Lots of singing was and is done at the lahal games too. My uncle Paul and grandfather Frank really loved to play and sing. I'm like that now too. I even sing the funeral songs cause my mom made me stand with her, Pleasa, and Josephine Bob at the funerals and told me that would be my job when I got older. I didn't believe her but now here I am! (personal communication, November 25, 2010)

As Kristy described, Hand Drumming has been a very long-standing tradition of the Secwépemc people and others. We are thankful that the practice was not wiped out when our cultural practices were banned under the Indian Act from 1884 to 1951. For me, the Hand Drum represents the connection between humans, earth, and the circle of life. As I reconnected to my homeland, my second drum (see Figure 2.1) was gifted to me by the education director in my T'exelc community for a conference presentation in Cairns, Australia, in 2010.

My theoretical framework was channelled through my first Hand Drum. My cultural reawakening began with the celebration of Secwépemc Knowledge through the handling of my Hand Drum; my Hand Drum is what constitutes

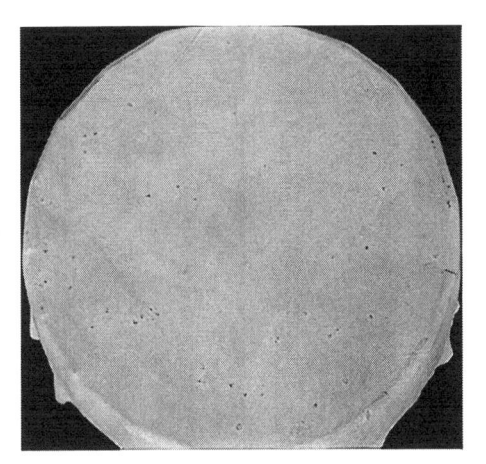

Figure 2.1 Top and bottom of the Hand Drum gifted by my nation. | Courtesy Georgina Martin

a critical relationship with my Indigenous ontology. My Hand Drum was gifted to me by my lifelong friend Lena Paul from my Secwépemc community. I, in return, acknowledged and accepted the responsibilities of owning the Hand Drum. The gifting is not taken lightly. I was reminded of the stories my grandparents told to me about how men and women in the community were observed and selected for important leadership or community roles by the way they presented themselves, from childhood through adolescence. Future leaders are selected through the performance of critical leadership qualities such as humility, honesty, respect, responsibility, and good character.

In 2002, my friend gifted me with the Hand Drum because she felt that I was ready to receive it. By accepting the Hand Drum, I agreed to honour, respect, and care for the drum. I was not certain about the meaning and magnitude of the gift, although I was willing to learn; I came to realize the sacredness of the Hand Drum and its significance to Secwépemc culture. The passing on and acceptance of the Hand Drum is in itself a story. The first drum I acquired was not simply given to me; rather, the presenter, my friend Lena Paul, commissioned the making of the drum from Herman Paul and then prepared for the most appropriate moment to present me with the drum. The exchange of the drum is a reciprocal honouring between the giver and the receiver and it carries spiritual and sacred value: the Hand Drum is not an object, it is alive and breathes life.

The finished and gifted Hand Drum (Figure 2.2) reminded me of my identity at the beginning of my studies.

Figure 2.2 My First Secwépemc Hand Drum. | Courtesy Georgina Martin

First, when I was gifted with the drum, the drum represented how I felt about my identity at that place and time; from there, I learned how to use the Hand Drum with a song; then, as I became more acquainted with Hand Drumming, I learned more about appreciating and honouring the assembly of the drum with all its parts. I have come to realize all the necessary steps to tender care and protection for our precious cultural representations. These feelings felt inherent when I made my own Hand Drum, wove baskets out of pine needles, and in 2020, made a rattle from elk hide. Through the connection with our cultural traditions and values, I experienced equivalent processes as I presented what has shaped my and my participants' identities. The graphic representation of the Hand Drum in figure 2.3 serves as my theoretical framework, which helps me recreate and maintain linkages with my cultural beginnings.

The Hand Drum guided me in my search to unravel the value and sacredness of identities. I began with the handle of the Hand Drum. The handle is woven with sinew in the shape of a spider web; this handle signifies my intertwining relationships.[1] This web configuration aligns with Absolon's (2011, 31) representation of how "Indigenous worldviews teach people to see themselves humbly within a larger web or circle of life." The relevance of this representation is not only how I connect with the drum but also how I feel very connected to

HUMILITY

Home   *Identity*

HONOUR   *Stories*   *Teachings*   HOPE

Handle: represents the grandparents I hung on to.

Experiences   *Indigenous Knowledge*

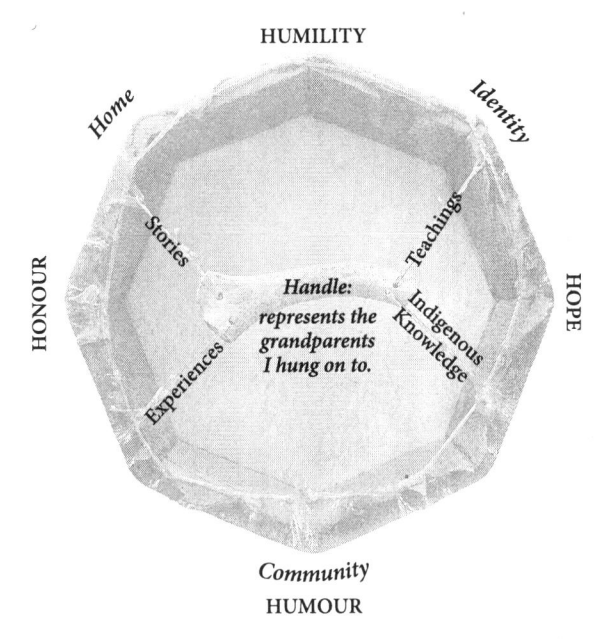

Community
HUMOUR

Figure 2.3 Understanding the Hand Drum as guide and metaphor for my inquiry. | Courtesy Georgina Martin

my homeland. The webbed handle "contains our relationships to one another and all of Creation" (Absolon 2011, 31). I connected with the Hand Drum to help me to understand and articulate the important Secwépemc qualities I grew up with, including honour, humility, hope, and humour.

The handle contains the memories that keep me connected to my grandparents. The spiritual connection I regained represents the knowledge I acquired from the relationships I had growing up with them and the depth of these connections; Leilani Holmes (2000, 46) refers to this as "heart knowledge." She explains that the knowledge passed on through the generations in her Hawaiian culture unites with the kupuna (Elders) of generations past in a relationship known as "blood memory." My memories are what sustain my heart knowledge and blood memory with my grandparents. The sinew straps that anchor the handle of the drum represents my lived experiences, Indigenous Knowledge, teachings, and the stories that keep me connected to my identities. My memories hold the key to my cultural rootedness and they help me realize how my lived experiences connect me with the cultural teachings of my grandparents. The Hand Drum itself helps me find direction in the meaning-making; the graphic also shows how I went about my research using an Indigenous Knowledge paradigm – incorporating honour, humility, hope, and humour.

The Handle – My Grandparents

In my memory, my grandparents are vivid. They were the most important people in my life growing up. My connection to them is so strong that I can return to times and places and relive the feelings and emotions I felt then in the present moment. John Dewey (1938, 44) described the reliving of such experiences, and I connected with his reference to longitudinal and lateral connections:

> As an individual passes from one situation to another, his world, his environment, expands and contracts. He does not find himself living in another world but in a different part or aspect of one and the same world. What he has learned in the way of knowledge and skill in one situation becomes an instrument of understanding and dealing effectively with the situation to follow. The process goes on as long as life and learning continue.

Every part of the learning I gained from my grandparents' teachings continues in various forms and I constantly bring the teachings forward in my present life. Therefore, the connections with my grandparents became the starting place for my study and I rely on them in my narratives. As a result, these meaningful relationships represent who I became and how I will live out my future.

Experiences
I experience the values of my grandparents' teachings and I am reminded of the depth of our culture; although I am not completely connected to the culture, I feel its strength. I have many memories of times spent with my grandparents as a child, and they are only good. I remember particularly the strong work ethic my grandfather taught me. We lived in the T'exelc community in a one-room log house with an attic built by my grandfather. My grandparents and I slept on the main floor's living quarters, and the attic could provide temporary accommodation and was the space my grandmother used to dry choke cherries.

During the early 1960s, homes on the reservation had no indoor plumbing. My regular chores were collecting water for household use and carrying wood for the fire. At first, I would cart water in a bucket from the creek across the reserve and down over the hill. Because I was a child, it seemed far. Without indoor plumbing, water had to be carried for multiple uses like food preparation and cleaning. I can picture the water pails in their place, close by the wash basin and mirror for cooking and washing up. Later on, cold water pumps were placed in the community, making water more accessible and a lot closer to my grandparents' house. I collected wood from the woodpile outside the house where it was chopped by my grandpa or one of my uncles. The wood was carried inside the house and placed in the wood box alongside, but not too close to, the stoves. We had two stoves, one for cooking and the other for heat. These memories are the voices that connect me back to my grandparents.

I loved doing my chores because when I finished, I would sit patiently by my grandpa on his bedside until he gave me the nod to pull the cardboard box out from underneath his bed to find my treat. I could choose from apples, oranges, or dried fruit, which my grandpa called "ears." To this day, dried apricots are my favourite dried fruit. The reward system worked well for me, training me to earn my way.

Equally valuable are the experiences I shared with my grandmother. I remember when I accompanied her on berry-picking trips. Depending on the season and place, we gathered Saskatoon berries, wild currants, gooseberries, cranberries, and choke cherries. Now, in my memory, I can hear the sounds and smell the savoury scent of the Saskatoon berries boiling on the stovetop as they were prepared for pies. Choke cherries were dried on paper in the attic for winter consumption. If it wasn't the sweetness of berries in the air, it was the strong odour from the preparation of moose or deer hides. The odour depended on the preserving stage of the hide. If it was at the beginning, it would be the smell of the hide mixed with brains from the animal, which was not very pleasant. The cured hides were used for making moccasins, gloves, or jackets, which had a very pleasant smoked smell. As I revisited these memories, I realized that for me to understand my experiences from my identity losses, I must travel back to my stories, such as these, and interrogate the experiences that disrupted my connection.

Indigenous Knowledge
By applying a culturally relevant framework, Lester Rigney (1999, 117, as cited in Smith 2005, 87) explains, Indigenous researchers can disrupt the "history of exploitation, suspicion, misunderstanding, and prejudice of indigenous peoples in order to develop methodologies and approaches to research that privilege indigenous knowledges, voices, experiences, reflections, and analyses of their social, material and spiritual conditions." It was important that my research utilized methodologies that privileged Jean's, Colten's, and my voice through the sharing of personal stories and connections to our Indigeneity.

I agree with Sandy Grande (2008, 236) that "Native students and educators deserve a pedagogy that cultivates a sense of collective agency as well as a praxis that targets the dismantling of colonialism ... it is one of our primary responsibilities as educators to link the lived experience of theorizing to the processes of self-recovery and social transformation." In addition to the transformational power of Indigenous Knowledge, the powerful stories awaken the conscience; both the cognitive and affective domains are moved. The stories told promote the transformation of both the storytellers and the story readers. Therefore, the transformation of mindsets balanced the delicate nature of the healing journey that evolved. Through the process, I found safety within autobiography, and the practical application of Indigenous Knowledge became prevalent. Indigenous Knowledge was built around the memories I retained of my grandparents; these memories connect me spiritually to my homeland, my grandparents' teachings, and now to my Hand Drum too.

Teaching and Stories

The teachings from my grandparents proved to be extremely valuable as I brought them forward from adolescence into adulthood. I often wondered how others were taught in their homes and if learning from grandparents shaped the experience of other children in other households. I did not spend much time with other families. According to my memory, I was mainly alone with my grandparents, so I cannot determine if other children were taught the way I was. While growing up, I did not wonder about how other children were taught. Now, later in life, I do. My inquiry into identities transformed me from my head to my heart, which reflected a process of reconciliation (truth telling) of inner struggles to integrate the teachings and words of my grandfather, especially his imperative to never forget where I come from. I return to the notion of "never to forget where you come from" because it is circular and it is conducive to our Secwépemc ways.

I remember hearing stories about relatives and friends who travelled from village to village. The trip would take days, sometimes weeks, by horse and wagon depending on the distance. When the travellers arrived in the village, they were received and greeted with courtesy. My grandfather spoke about how meals would be prepared for the travellers and how they would be served food first. This was a teaching that I remember. In terms of proper protocol and etiquette, children were taught to wait while the guests were given priority. After the meal, the tables were cleared and the dishes washed while the guests rested. By listening to the stories of my grandfather, I knew what my role was when guests arrived, and I knew what I could expect when I travelled to a neighbouring community. Ron Ignace (2008) includes reciprocity as a feature of Secwépemc culture; he describes how invited guests knew it was tacitly understood that they would return the favour of hospitality at a later date. I found through my own research how reciprocity and several other Secwépemc cultural markers have faded or disappeared. The destructive forces will be exposed in subsequent chapters as Elder Jean's stories unfold. Traditional Knowledge gained from living alongside my grandparents shaped the stories that I have come to live by, they shaped my successes, and they also shaped who I have become and am still becoming. My identity formation was also influenced by observations of the practice of the four Hs in my community.

The Four Hs

The four Hs – *honour, humility, hope,* and *humour* – reverberate throughout our territory and demarcate the resilience and survivance of the Secwépemc peoples. The four Hs are empowering attributes for the Secwépemc and other Indigenous Nations as well. The first H – *honour* – extends to self, family, community, Elders, and the Creator. In my intergenerational study, Jean, Colten, and I collectively honour and uphold our grandparents as our trusted guides. Honour is the highest degree of respect that is passed on to esteemed Elders, parents, and important people in the community.

The second H – *humility* – includes self-respect and self-worth. It is a strong leadership quality. For example, many people in our community collectively work behind the scenes to support various community and cultural events. The silent and prominent leaders offer their skills and labour with diligence because they care about and are committed to successful outcomes. It is the extreme sense of being humble. Honour and humility are values that the Secwépemc carry out with the highest degree of reverence. They walk through life with humility, and they do not expect any form of recognition. People may or may not be honoured but it is something they do not seek. The three of us collectively and continuously honour our grandparents through our humility.

The third H – *hope* – is necessary for survival or survivance. There is always hope that our lives and our futures will improve. Without the sense of hope for progress, living would feel insurmountable. Hope helps to turn darkness into possibilities. We have hope that our cultures will thrive. Through lessons learned from grandparents and Elders, I uncovered that the Secwépemc have an innate sense of who they are. The hope for advancement and improved socioeconomic conditions as more Indigenous students obtain degrees is another example.

The fourth H – *humour* – is our saving grace. Humour helps us endure and live through difficult situations. Humour is healing. For example, rather than feeling overcome by grief when faced with difficulties, humour helps us cope with feelings of loss or helplessness, making the situation more manageable. I believe humour helped us remain resilient to survive the residential school experiences and other cultural and social atrocities. If it was not for the healing power of humour, I believe that many more of us would have been consumed by the onslaught of trauma caused by the separation from language, families, and communities. Many of us are thankful that the healing power of humour massaged our spirits and kept us strong. The four Hs are values that many Indigenous Peoples continue to live by today.

The Spirit of the Hand Drum

Prior to my own drumming experience, I witnessed Secwépemc people Hand Drumming at many community and cultural events. I noted how drummers would honour the Hand Drum; the drummers would set aside any feelings of negativity before taking their place in the drumming circle. This must be genuine and authentic because the power of the drum is felt and carried through the group. No one wields power over the other; everyone is on an equal footing and negativity is dispelled. The dispelling of negativity can occur months/weeks/days/minutes before the event, depending on when the person is approached or when they decide to drum. The request for drummers can be made by approaching the person and offering tobacco or, in places like UBC, a call for drummers is made and the drummers are acknowledged by some form of gifting. When the drummer agrees to drum, they begin to plan by thinking about the ceremony and the context they will be part of. The request for and acceptance of participation has its own cultural protocols. I recognized that the practice of drumming is powerful because I learned that the spirit people are present to help. The power of the Hand Drum is shown in the power and unity of the community. The same principle and cultural protocols are applied during sharing and healing circles. At the outset, I was fearful that I did not qualify to handle the Hand Drum, but as I became stronger, I realized that this fear was causing my reluctance to participate. It was only through the encouragement of Elders Jean William, Florence James, and Delores Louie that I managed to achieve the level of strength I have today.

A good example of the power of the drum can be found in the work of Kim Anderson (2000), a Métis scholar who described how Edna Manitowabi felt when she first heard the drum. Manitowabi is Odawa/Ojibway from Wikwemikong, Manitoulin Island, and head woman for the Eastern Doorway of the Three Fires Midewewin Lodge. She is well-known nationally as a traditional teacher, ceremonialist, drum keeper, and grandmother. She has been instrumental in the re-introduction of traditional teachings and ceremonies in her local area, and she is an active researcher of traditional medicines. Manitowabi said the drum reached inside her, giving her "a great sense of peace," and a feeling of "coming home to where I belonged" (142). The drum deepened the emotion in her heart and awakened her spirit. It brought the memories of her grandmothers, grandfathers, and ancestors: historical and blood memory. Manitowabi related to the sound of the little boy water drum: it gave her strength. This drum is central to Indigenous cultures in Eastern Canada; I first heard the sound of the little boy water drum in Peterborough, Ontario. Native drumming can help women dismantle negative definitions of being and lead them to places where they will find powerful affirmations of self and nation (143). My Hand Drum is guiding my spiritual path because it amplifies the voices of my ancestors. The drum is also healing. There are many facets to Secwépemc culture, but the Hand Drum is the most central for me at this time.

Before I connected with my Hand Drum, the spiritual realm was missing in everything I did. Now, as I drum, I appreciate Eugene Richard Atleo's (2004, xi) concept of Nuu-chah-nulth Indigenous Knowledge as the inclusivity of all reality, physical and metaphysical; everything being one. Accordingly, Nuu-chah-nulth origin stories predate "the conscious historical notion of civilization and scientific progress." Like metaphysicality, Archibald's (2008) holism represents the circle of life; there is no perceived beginning and no perceived end. All the parts are interrelated and equally important. In my relational sphere, self is at the centre and inclusive of, and extending to, family, community, Elders, spiritual guidance, and the Creator. It is necessary to be at one with one's self to embrace the connection to Indigenous Knowledge. Without knowing oneself within a Secwépemc ontological relationship, the individual, like me, will feel a defective sense of genealogy.

Therefore, due to the magnitude of my identity scope, it was difficult to problematize identity. It became a challenge to unpack and repack the meanings of identities. To help me relate to and situate my topic, I reflected on Joyce Schneider's (2007, 6) description of her separation from identities. She wrote:

The separation inflicted upon my community by the residential school system, the dispossession of our lands and rights to govern ourselves using our own laws and ways of being has resulted in our alienation from each other, our territory (for many of us) and our rightful inheritance to our language, stories, and vital connections to past, present, and future family members.

In the same year, I (2007, 14) wrote about the loss of identity from a political science viewpoint:

The loss of identity is a major threat to the loss of a people because it severs individual identity from community and culture. The formation of identity is by language, custom, tradition and practice. Therefore, the loss of culture and identity eradicates the Aboriginal continuum. Aboriginal youth are especially threatened by loss of culture if they replace hunting, trapping and fishing by opportunities to get a driver's licence, chat on the internet, and pursue contemporary trends. This reality will continue as Aboriginal people migrate to urban centres and youth either lose touch with their homeland or do not develop communal and cultural roots.

I recognize that our identities and collective cohesion are fragile. Like Beatrice Marie Anderson, I feel the outrage, hurt, and pain of colonial impositions. Anderson (2011, 8) asks, "When will we be heard?"; she then declares that we must transform to regain and revitalize Indigenous languages, cultures, families, and communities for our continued survival.

I felt confused and wondered about my identities. Memories return from when I was a young child, maybe around six. I heard my grandfather's words and I set out to follow them. He said that I needed to go out (leave the community) and get an education and bring it back to our people, and I was never to forget who I am and where I come from. The words my grandfather spoke to me so many years ago continue to resonate. I remember them clearly to this day. I am astounded at the profound effect his words carry. He had no formal Western-oriented education; he was the steward of life-teachings necessary for the survival of our people. I could not fully understand what it meant to bring education back to the people, so by undertaking my doctoral research in collaboration with my community I hope I have accomplished what my grandfather wished. Through my research focus on the lives of three generations of Secwépemc people, I am interested in what shaped and challenged the development and sustenance of Secwépemc identities. Of particular interest are Secwépemc culture, identities, and worldviews, all of which are explored in the forthcoming chapters.

The Drum Is Connected to the Land

My Secwépemc Hand Drum extends from the spirit of the land through its physical properties – the drum's surface is made from deer hide and the wooden frame is made from cedar. In my heritage, our connectedness to the land is acknowledged and the Secwépemc people respect how the moose or deer sacrifice their hide and they pay homage to the animals' spirits. The trees are also important in my culture, providing shelter, medicine, and transportation. They are sources of nourishment, and their roots represent our rootedness to the earth. These are important elements for survival, and they are directly linked to Mother Earth.

Equally linked to Mother Earth is the sound of the drum. It was explained to me that when all the Hand Drummers are in sync, their synchronization resonates with the heartbeat of Mother Earth. There is no short cut or quick way to learn how to reach this moment; the experienced Hand Drummer will simply feel it. Ultimately, the sacredness of the Hand Drum commands honour and integrity. Therefore, my acceptance of the Hand Drum bestowed on me the responsibility to care for it and use it in a good way. Similarly, the sacredness of the Hand Drum correlates with the highest degree of care necessary when I handle the stories I have been gifted. The release of the stories demands crucial curatorship to ensure their truth is honoured.

Connecting to Indigenous Knowledge

To connect with and embrace Indigenous Knowledge, I reflected on the trickster story "Coyote Searching for the Bone Needle," shared by Archibald (2008, 35–36), who heard it from Eber Hampton of the Chickasaw Nation. The story resonated with Archibald because Hampton made connections between motives and methods in storytelling, as shown in this paradigmatic example:

> In the story, Old Man Coyote was searching for a bone needle by the fire and Owl showed up to help. Owl told Old Man Coyote that the needle could not be found around the fire; if it had been there, Owl would have spotted it. Old Man Coyote told Owl that the needle was used quite a ways over in the bushes. Owl wondered why Old Man Coyote was looking by the fire then Old Man Coyote explained that it was easier to see by the fire because it gave off good light.

In essence, I am searching for my own bone needle, like Old Man Coyote. This paradigmatic example helps me ponder my lived experiences and the teachings or theory of the teachings from my grandparents and Elders to unravel the underpinnings of Indigenous Knowledge. Like Old Man Coyote, I must figure out where to look before I begin my search, otherwise I could make the mistake of looking in the wrong places, like he did. The desired outcome was to make meaning of my own story. The search, through my dissertation work, helped me understand my life. The channelling of my way home through academia is a huge part of me and a part of my Hand Drum. The delicate balance required to reconcile Indigenous and Western worldviews is expressed in Owl questioning why Old Man Coyote is searching for the bone needle by the fire. Owl confirms that the bone needle is not there because he would have spotted it. I understand from this message that Owl is cautioning Old Man Coyote not to look in the wrong places. Therefore, I must ensure that I do not become confused and distort my articulation of Secwépemc worldviews. I must listen carefully and pay attention to the teachings and values. The assuredness of Owl's statement coincides with Archibald's (2008) advice that by listening and watching we gain understanding from the Elders before we make meaning of their words. The interpretation of stories carries the same responsibility; before the storyteller can make meaning of the story, they must listen intuitively to ensure the essence of the story is correct; a change in the wording could change the whole story. This approach, Archibald explains, is an important element of story sharing; it allows the listener (who becomes the reader when the stories are written down) to make meaning of the words and stories without direction from the storyteller (meaning-making). This challenge is conveyed when Owl wonders why Old Man Coyote is looking by the fire and it turns out that it was because it is easier to see by the fire. Therefore, to convey the truth and co-construct participant stories, one must move away from the fire and really listen with our eyes and our ears. Each time I wonder if I am hearing correctly, I reflect on the transmission of Archibald's (2008) teachings from the Elders, my grandfather's voice, and the beat of the Hand Drum. Each of these elements, in harmony, represents the heartbeat of Mother Earth as well. I felt comfortable with the Hand Drum as my foundation because I am in my formative years as a Drummer and Hand Drumming is pivotal to our culture.

The multiple layers of meaning created by the Owl and Coyote trickster story is one example of how Indigenous scholars utilize story to create new Indigenous Knowledge pedagogy and make meaning of Traditional Knowledge. New meaning depends on the purpose of the interpretation, how the story is told by the storyteller, and how it is received by the listener. As I developed my research focus on identities, I searched for my own bone needle. My thoughts and reflections are circular; they bring me back to how I was taught and the important words of my grandfather, who continued to remind me to never forget where I come from. The respectful words of my grandfather give me guidance and I honour them.

Wilson (2008, 33) shares that Indigenous Knowledge and Secwépemc ways of knowing can be understood as "the theory of how we come to have knowledge, or how we know something." He continues:

> It includes entire systems of thinking or styles of cognitive functioning that are built upon specific ontologies. Epistemology is tied in to ontology, in that what I believe to be "real" is going to impact on the way that I think about that "reality." Choices made about what is "real" will depend upon how your thinking works and how you know the world around you.

By sharing the development, over time, of my ways of knowing, I offer a narrative of growing awareness: mine. My personal reflection has uncovered my epistemological knowledge, learned through the teachings of my grandparents.

Moving from My Head to My Heart

The longest journey we will ever make is from our head to our heart.
• ELDER BOB CARDINAL, ENOCH, ALBERTA

To advance a proactive agenda, I needed the strength and determination to move from my head to my heart. I chose Archibald's *Indigenous Storywork: Educating the Heart, Mind, Body, and Spirit* (2008) to show care and appreciation for the sharing and telling of Elder Jean's and Colten's stories. The storywork approach established by Archibald shifted my writing style from linear to circular storytelling. Allow me to explain what this means.

Archibald (2008, 108) began by establishing relationships as she took direction from Elders based "on the fundamental values of respect, reverence, responsibility, and reciprocity." Archibald explained the cultural readiness required when interacting with Elders. I adhered to the same respect and cultural readiness by honouring Elder Jean. I met with her at her home and then I continually followed up with her. I applied the same principle of storytelling in my communication with Colten by spending time with him in places where he felt comfortable. When I articulated my own story, I reverted to narrative inquiry because this approach helped me to invoke memories from my lived experience. Similar to Trudy Cardinal (2010), I needed to understand my lived experience before I could explore Jean's and Colten's identities. Cardinal demonstrates how narrative inquiry helps the writer deepen their understanding of their lived experiences; this was crucial for me as I worked through the struggle of my loss of identities. I became increasingly aware of the effects of these losses. In concert with the two story-sharing and -telling genres (Indigenous storywork and narrative inquiry), I moved from my head to my heart. The care of stories is succinctly expressed by Sean Michael Lessard (2010, 22): "Narrative inquiry helps me respect the individual within the research and attends to the details of a life because it provides space for the experience and honours the inquiry process." I positioned myself by using the same approach as Lessard. He adds, "I wrote the stories with spirituality in mind and reflecting on the importance of taking care of a story" (32). Lessard found that he had to attend to one of his participant's stories differently because of his relationship with her family. Similarly, I considered my position with the community and my relationality with the participants so I could attend to the intricacies of sharing stories truthfully.

Scraping and Removing the Fur to See and Hear the Drum

The complexity of identities parallels the complexity of preparing the deer or moose hide for the creation of the Hand Drum. It begins with the scraping and removing of the fur from the hide, which, as I noted earlier, is very delicate work. In the drum-making process, I understood how the animal hair is removed from the hide and how, if the hide is not handled with extreme care, it could be nicked, destroying that part of the hide. I equate the preparation of the deer or moose hide to my own preparation for understanding the participants' stories before I released them. I prepared myself by remembering the delicate care given to the hide as it is scraped with a sharp tool to remove the hair, fat, and blood and smooth out the roughness in the hide. The first precaution prior to handling the hide is recognizing the appropriate time of year to take the hide from the animal. For example, a hide taken in the spring would be too thin for drum-making because the animal is lean. After the hide receives its final rinse; it is rolled into a ball and placed in the freezer for preserving until the drum frame is ready. The preserving of the hide corresponds to the time required to honour and portray the stories. When the stories are transmitted from teller to listener, they are not interpreted immediately; rather, the listener invests time in reflecting on the stories to ensure the meaning is accurate. The presence of the Hand Drum reminds me to devote the necessary care and attention to the meaning of stories.

I made an ethical and positive shift to reframe my thoughts about identities through stories, reflecting on what Mary Isabelle Young (2003, 53) said about language and identity: "Not knowing my language I feel like a mute in the world [and yet] I know where I am, and I know that I belong [here]." I experience the same mute feelings, yet I know I belong too; I want to help other people, ethically and responsibly, to help sort out where we all belong.

The Hand Drum helped me spiritually to confront the harmful identity disruptions caused by colonialism, forced assimilation, residential schools, and the Indian Act so I could have a clearer frame of reference. I was able to navigate my educational experience between Secwépemc teachings and Western knowledge. In 2008, I was fortunate to have the opportunity to practice my culture by beginning to learn how to Hand Drum. This critical experience taught me to connect heart, mind, body, and spirit. My connectedness to the Hand Drum is powerful and sacred; this is what grounds me. I know this from personal experience as an aspiring Hand Drummer. We are very fortunate that although our practices were outlawed, they were sustained. I am able to recall the importance of Hand Drumming from my embodied memories during childhood. It is this inherent knowledge that leads me back to the important practice of the Hand Drum. Very little has been documented about Hand Drumming. The early explorers and missionaries held a low opinion of our cultural practice, calling it "barbaric" (Goudreau et al. 2008, 72). While cultural practices were banned from 1884 to 1951, many communities were vigilant and innovative in their ways of cultivating and retaining these practices by going underground. In similar fashion to my childhood memories, the practice of Hand Drumming emerged from cell memory. It is a testament to the resilience of Indigenous Peoples that we hung on to our practices, and many people have proudly reclaimed them.

Integrating my cultural awakening, my grandparents' teachings, and my journey through academia represents my version of the beat of the drum keeping time with the heartbeat of Mother Earth. My Hand Drum is my catalyst: to anchor me and awaken my spirit. As I go forward, I am always remembering the words of my grandfather to "never forget where I come from."

CHAPTER 3

Honouring the Drummer: Embodied Knowledge from within My Community

Weyt-kp, Georgina Ren skwekwst, Secwépemc-ken te T'exelc re st'e7e7kwen.
Hello everyone, Georgina is my name. I come from T'exelc.
Re Secwépemc wenecwem re stsgwey ell tukwentus re sxyemstwecws.
The Secwépemc should honour, humility and also love to show humour.
- ELDER JEAN WILLIAM, 2012

Announcing Myself

For many years, I have engaged with serious deep reflection on the feelings I continue to harbour. The sense that I am not good enough or that I'm lost have affected me for years. When I feel down, I often call on my ancestors and grandparents to help me think clearly while I drum songs for strength and support. To this day, I remain uncertain about where these deep-rooted discomforts and disconnections began in my earlier years, though I now recognize that the emotional, physical, psychological, and spiritual losses caused by the absence of my mother throughout my formative years are an important part of this. I am sure this loss transformed into self-doubt about my being. Throughout my life I carried this with me, and it caused me to reflect on how my story could be important. I have continued to gain strength in my reconnections as I opened this chapter with a quote from Elder Jean in the Secwepemctsín language to announce myself and where I come from. The remaining translation in the quote captures the meaning of honour, humility, and humour in its closest form. I have offered the closest literal translation in the language. Francis Lee Brown's (2004, 4) words gave me consolation when he said, "Emotions provide energy for learning that is activated through perception, creating the possibility of thought and understanding. Without emotions, there is no thought, no learning, no education, no research, no dreams and no conscious life. In Native symbology emotions are represented, at times, as water."

These words helped me to understand how the flow of energy, emotion, and water helps one to recognize the importance of understanding the emotional losses that a person experiences during childhood. I realized that without the wholeness of mind, body, and spirit, I will continue to experience the absence of learning. I agree that "there is a need to understand the colonization of Aboriginal emotion in order to develop an understanding of how to regain the emotional maturity for de-colonization" (Brown, 2004, 17). Maybe I am so colonized that I will continue to search for validation, and quite often this causes my confidence to remain shaky. I know that I am a victim of the historical emotional trauma I experienced from being separated from one of the most important people in my life, my mother. According to Brown, "A natural relationship between any two human beings is defined by loving affection, communication and cooperation. However, the special human capacity for relational response can be interrupted or suspended by an experience of physical or emotional distress" (76). My story is about feeling the absence of affection and realizing how my lived experiences of interruption and suspension of emotions bred anguish. My story begins.

My Humble Beginnings

My name is Georgina Rose Martin (née Wycotte) and my birthplace is the Coqualeetza Indian Hospital in Sardis, BC. I was born into a family of five girls and four boys, and I am the middle child. At the time of this writing, there were seven of us left. The main village where I grew up is approximately one-quarter of a kilometre off Highway 97 on the right driving south from Williams Lake toward Vancouver. The house where I lived with my grandparents was the third house on the left as you drove into the original part of the community. My uncle's house was tucked in behind the second house.

To situate the beginning of my story, I reflect on my personal interview conducted on April 20, 2010, moderated by a fellow student in an Institutional Ethnography course taught by Dorothy E. Smith. The course exercise gave me the opportunity to begin an experiential account of my given topic: identity. I confirmed my direction by exploring how identity personally impacts me.

While I continued to write my autobiography, I moved between the three-dimensional inquiry spaces outlined by Clandinin and Connelly (2000) which are: the personal and social (interaction); past, present, and future (continuity); and place (situation). I also move inward, outward, backward, and forward as I tell and retell my stories. These stories consist of my personal lived experiences growing up in my community of T'exelc and they are told from my perspective.

In my memory, I have no recollection of having any emotional connections or of being held or hugged much, if at all. The physical and emotional contact was just not apparent while I was growing up. I wondered if this practice was absent from all families because I heard other people later in life talk about how physical affection was not really practised. The missing display of affection became a real problem because it is an ongoing legacy; I rarely felt healthy physical affection, so I am not able to pass it forward to my children, which is very painful. Today, I am not very good at hugging. I do remember a significant person other than my grandparents in my life growing up that helped me feel special and that was my uncle Ken. In his presence, I felt important. Slipping back in time, I explore memories of my life with my grandparents by beginning with the story of my grandparents' photograph.

The Story of My Grandparents' Photo

In July 2009, as I read the course requirements for a graduate course on narrative inquiry at the Building Peaceful Communities Summer Institute in Edmonton, Alberta, I realized that I needed a photograph or artifact that had special meaning. Without hesitation, I chose the picture of my grandparents, likely because I knew my grandparents cared for me and an objective of the course was to understand identity-making as relational practices. I carefully wrapped the photo and tucked it into my travel bag as I prepared to drive from Prince George to Edmonton, a 738 kilometre drive east. I have many photographs of my family, yet the photograph of my grandparents is the one I selected without hesitation. On the morning we were to share the photograph, I carefully carried the photograph in my special scarf into the Centre for Research for Teacher Education and Development and into the small office where I met with Colleen and Lynne, the two other members of my research circle group. Even though we had only known each other for a few days, we often shared our feelings, reaching for the box of tissue nearby. I knew the photograph would generate deep feelings in me, therefore I needed to be emotionally

Figure 3.1 Ned and Nancy Moiese, Georgina's grandparents. | Courtesy Georgina Martin

prepared for the events ahead. Each time I have intimate reflection with my grandparents in their photograph I have difficulty containing my emotions. I do much better now because I feel that they are always looking out for me. I cannot explain why I have such deep sad emotions because my memories of my grandparents are sacred; maybe the emotion is connected to my own feelings of loss that I felt when they passed on. I handled the photograph carefully and spoke about how it is one of the few items I acquired when my grandfather passed on. Rather than asking the reader to flip back to the early pages of the book, I reshare my cherished photo here, in Figure 3.1.

While I spoke with Lynne and Colleen, tears welled up in my eyes as I gazed at the photograph of my grandparents with their arms wrapped around each other's shoulders. I noticed how they looked very happy, a young couple, possibly in their thirties. Yet my grandfather looks tired. I am not sure what type of work he did, but I know by the values he passed on to me that he was a hard-working man. As Lynne, Colleen, and I sat together, I looked at the photo and directly into my grandparents' eyes. The photograph is in colour, although there is a section on my grandmother's left where there is black and white coming through. I learned that, in earlier days of photography, photographs were taken in black and white and the colour was painted in. I told

Lynne and Colleen that I still hold my grandparents in high esteem; they were the most important people in my life growing up. For as long as I can remember, my grandparents raised me. As I gaze at my grandmother now, I see myself in her. I never realized this connection before; maybe I am beginning to get closer to who I am and who I am becoming, through self-acceptance. They don't have big smiles, yet I see them as content. My grandpa is handsome, and my grandma is beautiful. All I could say were good things about my grandparents because I cherish them, as I do their photo. I spoke to how they took care of me while I was in their care. They gave me all the essentials, and I was taught moral values including a strong work ethic and the importance of being kind to others and having good character. In relation to good character, they taught me that I must remember that, when I am out in the world, people are watching and noticing and I must behave well because I represent my family and my community. This is the good character teaching to ensure that I did my best to carry and uphold respect for my family and community. I may not have lived up to all the things I was taught, but my grandparents gave me a very strong foundation that I return to often. I spoke of how my grandparents gave me special gifts by teaching me to be principled and, most importantly, to have a strong work ethic. For these gifts I am very grateful to my grandparents; they built a very strong foundation.

I shared the reason I lived with my grandparents with Lynne and Colleen. I told them I knew that my mom was quarantined in an Indian hospital with tuberculosis. I have not researched the events surrounding my birth yet; I am not quite prepared for the emotional challenges that precede exploring the unknown. I feel that the less I know at the moment helps me to disassociate from the pain of not being close to my mother. This feeling is an ongoing life experience. I have participated in many healing seminars and programs over the years to address unresolved childhood detachment issues. On June 24, 1990, I wrote a letter to my mom. In the letter, I spoke of the importance of love and affection. I said, "To me that [love] is very important otherwise you grow up empty and displaced." The letter was written to help me move through emotions associated with the feelings of loss. I was likely exploring the sense of connection at this time because my youngest daughter was born in March of the same year. Understanding the imbalance that resulted from the separation and how to heal is imperative for me if I am to gain the ability to help my children heal from intergenerational trauma. I realize I must arrest the feelings of displacement if I am to avoid passing them on. To this day, the expression of affection is a work in progress.

Living the Stories of My Photograph
Because I shared the photograph as part of my inquiry process, Lynne and Colleen began to ask me questions and wondered with me within the three-dimensional spaces – that is, within the dimensions of temporality, sociality, and place. Together, we wondered about where the photograph was taken and the events that were going on around that time. It looks like a posed photograph, and we wondered if a commercial photographer had come to where we lived and offered his services. Or perhaps it was a special occasion. I realized I did not know why it was taken, or where, or what events were going on around that time. I knew that they were not wearing their everyday clothes because I remembered my grandfather's blue jeans and my grandmother's dresses. Sliding backward in time, together we wondered why I was the only one of nine children to stay with my maternal grandparents. Each time I go through these wonderings, raw emotion surfaces and I cry. I wondered more about the tears, and I grappled with the memory that, through much of my upbringing, I also lived without my siblings too. Sliding backward to the stories of my birth, I wondered when the story of my living with my grandparents began. I wondered if I was with them when the photograph was taken. I wondered how old my mom was when the photograph was taken.

Through conversations with Elder Jean, I discovered that in our T'exelc community, family took care of family members. It was part of the system of caring that a young child was selected by grandparents so the grandchild would provide care when the grandparents needed help. I came to realize that it was not so surprising that I stayed with my grandparents after all. One of the stories I remember hearing is about my mom coming home. I was told that my grandparents decided to keep me and raise me as their own, so I must have been fairly young yet. To this day, I do not know when my mom recovered and was discharged from the Coqualeetza Indian Hospital. I still wonder. In conversation with Dr. Don Pratt at UBC about my identity exploration, I spoke of how my identity was shattered. I explained that I was taken directly from my mom at birth, and she was not allowed to hold me. He let out a shocked gasp, wondering how the separation from her newborn must have affected her. I was caught off guard by his response because I never considered how the separation could have affected my mom too. Until this conversation, it never crossed my mind that maybe she could have wanted me. I kept feeling rejection. I think about how taking care of family is part of the Secwépemc cultural narrative of my community and how it shapes all of our identities. As I think about the cost and responsibility of my grandparents having a child with them, I know that they always made me feel like I belonged with them, that I was wanted. Until I wrote about my grandparents' photograph, I did not pay attention to their age at the time. Now I realize that when I was five, my grandmother, according to the St. Joseph Oblate House records, would have been sixty-two and my grandpa sixty-three. They were by no means young to be raising a child from birth, but I must have brought joy into their lives.

I wondered again what occasioned the photograph. I remember that the photograph was always hung on the living room wall in a special place. When my grandfather passed on, I remembered the photograph and I acquired it. That was one of the most cherished items I wanted to keep. In January 2013, I discovered through conversation with my one remaining uncle that the photograph was taken when my grandparents attended Klondike night at the Elks Hall in Williams Lake. Having the photo helps me keep the spirit, teachings, and memories of my grandparents alive. I am not sure why I have the wrenching feeling of separation of not knowing who I am. I only need to look at my grandparents' photograph to remember that I did belong, and there were people who cared for me. Thinking about the larger social and cultural narratives, I wondered why my grandparents decided to spend the money that the photograph cost. I know their access to money was limited because my grandfather worked hard at manual labour. I know this because my grandpa could not read or write throughout his life so he would have to work with his hands to earn a living.

I wondered again if my grandparents lived in the same house where I lived with them when the photo was taken. Then I gaze at them in the photo, and I believe they are very strong and caring people. I tell myself a story that I inherited their strength. I admire them for passing it on to me; it has shaped my identity. It is the story I tell of who they were in my life that kept me strong and committed as I acquired my PhD. If I could tell my grandfather a story, I would tell him about my high school teachers encouraging me to continue on to university and how I did not feel that I was capable. I thought about this as I looked to the sky on my training run at the UBC track on April 5, 2013. I kept thinking, "It is really something that I am actually here at UBC right now." I never imagined ever being at this campus completing the highest degree possible. I honour and thank my grandparents for supporting me and training me to pursue something that I thought was impossible. I am sure they would be very proud to know that they planted the seed for me to pursue an education. I am very proud of them too, and I always will be.

A Story of Photographs: Where Are the Photographs of Me?

While I slipped back in time to reflect on photographs displayed in my grandparents' home, I remember only a few photos displayed in their home, and I realized there are no photographs of me at all in my childhood. I recall them being black-and-white photographs of relatives from the war, and another of a relative graduating from a registered nursing program. She was wearing her white nursing cap. Then, in later years there was another very special photograph, this of my uncle riding saddle bronc in the rodeo. There are no photographs of me in my infancy. I never saw my grandparents taking photographs; they never owned a camera, which would have been a luxury item at that time. My grandparents often spoke of the Great Depression, when everything including food was hard to come by. They were very frugal in their spending to ensure that food was a priority. The only photo I own from my earlier years is a group photo taken behind the day school I attended on the reserve (see Figure 3.2). I was seven when it was taken. This would be the first year of my primary education. The lack of photographs adds to the mystery of my childhood, not allowing me to create a clearer portrayal of my formative years.

Figure 3.2 Georgina in Grade 1. | Courtesy Georgina Martin

RETELLING THE STORIES

It was likely due to limited income that only photographs of very special occasions could be taken and displayed. Sliding back in time, I do not know of any baby or toddler photos of myself. I have no memory of my appearance as a young child or a visual of what was happening around me. I do have some recollection of how I was groomed and dressed after I started primary school. This could be another reason the photograph of my grandparents is a deeply cherished item, because there were no other photographs of them when they were young either.

The Red Hot Potbelly Stove

There is one strong childhood memory I have from when I was around three or four years old. At that point, my grandpa was sixty-two and my grandma sixty-one. I know it is a story I have told often. I do not remember if my grandma and grandpa ever told me the story of the Red Hot Stove, but I do remember the pain of the burn as my right arm made contact with the stove.

My grandparents called me "little mischief." I am not sure when they gave me the nickname, but I certainly remember that I fit the name on this particular day. I was behaving mischievously as I ran in circles around the Red Hot Potbelly Stove in the centre of our one-room log house. The stove was constructed from used gas or oil drums (large metal cans) at St. Joseph's Mission by men from our village who worked in the blacksmith shop at the school. St. Joseph's Mission was about a five-minute drive from our community. When I think about the institution, I know it had a lasting influence on our community. Many children from our village were taken from their families and sent to St. Joseph's Mission. The residential school had a strong mandate to assimilate beginning with the removal of children from their parents and extended family. The removal arrested the children's ability to learn and practice their traditional values of living off the land, of knowing their culture, and of speaking the Secwepemctsín language. The disconnection from families would be foreign for everyone. The students would see their siblings on the grounds of the residential school, but they were not permitted to speak with one another. For these brief periods, they could possibly exchange a few words or wave at each other. The disconnection wrought upon the children by the mission school caused family closeness and cohesion to fracture.

Returning to the story of the Potbelly Stove, on this particular day, the stove was very hot, giving off a bright red glow. As I ran around and around the stove, I can still see my grandpa from the corner of my left eye sitting on his bed in the corner of the room, telling me to "stop, you will fall on the stove and get burned." Over and over Grandpa repeated his words. He did not physically try to stop me. Perhaps he worried that if he moved toward me, I would become startled and lose my focus and my footing. True to my nickname, I did not listen to my grandpa's request, and I kept running clockwise. I do not know how long I did this, but I do remember slipping and falling on the Red Hot Stove. As I was running, with my right side facing the stove, I lost my grip and my feet gave way and my right shoulder touched the stove. The pain was intense, and I began to shriek and cry, and my grandpa jumped into action. I am not quite clear on how we got to the hospital in Williams Lake. My grandparents did not own a vehicle. My grandma and grandpa had very little money and neither of them had a driver's licence. I do not remember if my grandmother was in the house at the time nor do I remember if many people on the reserve owned vehicles.

Somehow, they got me to the hospital. I remember a white hospital located at the top of a hill. I cannot remember being treated. I heard people tell afterward that when I was being attended to, my grandparents heard me wailing from the pain and it bothered them. I am sure I was in great pain from falling on that Red Hot Stove. To this day, I have a scar on my right shoulder from the burn. The burn was quite large. Over the years, the scar has faded to the size of a loonie, but I will likely always wear this scar and remember the care that my grandparents had for me. I am grateful that my face did not touch the stove.

The Experience from the Fall
As I slide back to the time I fell on the Red Hot Stove, I can only think of how the incident must have affected my grandparents. From my memory, they were very gentle and caring people. I believe it was my grandfather's gentle nature that held him back from being abrupt, but it must have caused him grave anxiety to anticipate the inevitable. My grandfather always approached his teachings with noninterference. The task or information would be verbally conveyed, and it was up to me to do the rest. Following the incident, I am positive that they hurriedly found the means within the community to get me into the hospital in Williams Lake for medical attention. Perhaps my uncle, who owned a vehicle and lived a short distance from my grandparents, drove us there. If he was away from the community, it would be the caring and sharing nature of our people that would have allowed for a quick response to get me to a doctor. I am not sure if ambulances made trips from the City of Williams Lake to the reservation at that time.

Restorying brings forward memories and it was only when writing this story that I realized that when my colleague called me "trouble" it reminded me of "little mischief." I feel comfort with the nickname because it evokes emotions about the affection my grandparents gave me when they called me "little mischief." Perhaps the pain I associate with growing up and feeling disconnected comes from the lack of memories of being held or hugged; yet, I also remember how caring my grandparents were, how they were there for me and took care of my immediate needs in a nonphysical way. I can still feel the closeness I experienced spending time with both of my grandparents.

Retelling the Story – The Emotional Distance
It is from these earlier landscapes that I inherited the story that it was wrong to hold or hug loved ones. My grandma understood and displayed this behaviour as the traditional teachings of the Catholic Church in our community. It was frowned upon to have any physical contact with others, including family, because hugging was construed as a sexual fantasy. In this way, affection became a taboo. I recognize how the lack of physical contact affected my relationships in later years, especially with my children. In a letter I wrote to my eldest son on June 19, 1990, I said, "I did not learn how to feel or express my emotions. In turn I did not know how to do this with you ... I tried my best to be a mom. The things that hurt me when I was a little girl I tried to avoid repeating with you guys, and the things I needed I tried to give." I still cannot comfortably express affection. This was over thirty years ago, as of the time of this writing, and I still rarely have the courage to hug my children.

A Story of My Grandmother's Catholic Faith
Thinking about the absence of physical contact during my younger years, I realize that it must have stemmed from my grandmother's indoctrinated Catholicism. My grandma was a stoic Catholic; I remember accompanying her regularly to attend the Catholic Church on the reserve. She always helped out with special occasion events in the Catholic calendar, such as Easter and Christmas. Prior to Easter, we participated in the Signs of the Cross; I believe this began a week before Easter. I can hear my grandma lead the hymns and the singing of the rosary in English and Secwepemctsín. Church was an important event, and it was a priority for her. As a child, I had no choice; it was mandatory that I attend church with her. I do not recall my grandfather attending to the same degree, and I was not permitted to stay home with him either.

Because of my grandmother's attachment and devotion to the Catholic faith, we did not talk openly about personal matters like the female hormonal development; these conversations were sinful and therefore taboo. I was never prepared for any type of physical changes or development, and my physical changes were never explained; I only learned about the life cycle in my physical education classes in high school. The notion of sinful acts also influenced ideas about exposing the body, and it was abnormal to show our bodies; for example, the length of skirts was well below the knees, almost ankle length. When shorts were introduced, wearing shorts was not permitted at all until I was twelve, and then, the length had to remain below the knees, though eventually, shorts that fell to just above the knees were allowed. From childhood into my preadolescence, I fully respected both my grandparents and I adhered to their wishes. To this day, I continue to honour their memory; they were both very strong influences in my life as I grew up in their company.

My Tricycle Gift

I recollect the time I received a brand new tricycle as a Christmas gift from my uncle. I recall my age to be around two or three years old, so my grandpa was around fifty-nine and my grandma fifty-eight. I remember my uncle inviting me to his house, located close behind my grandparents' house. Funny, I do not recall the colour of my uncle's house, though; I think it was either light blue or white. When my uncle invited me to his house on that day, he said he had something to show me. I had no idea what it might be, but I recall being curious. As I entered the house, I remember a decorated Christmas tree to my right in the corner of the living room. As I slip back in time, I find this unusual because I had not noticed Christmas trees in other homes. My grandparents did not have a Christmas tree except for a small ornamental tree that sat on the kitchen table.

I was filled with excitement, anticipating what would happen next. I wanted to know what my uncle was being secretive about. He was behaving as if it was nothing unusual. My aunt was with us as well. As we passed through the living room, he told me to go ahead and look around. As I moved through the living room into the next room, my eyes lit up and I imagine they must have grown to the size of saucers. There was a pink tricycle. I looked at it and then at my uncle. "What are you waiting for?" he asked. "Get on the tricycle and try it out. It's for you." I never imagined owning a tricycle. In that moment, I was in awe. I felt very special. I got on the tricycle and rode it around the house. My uncle teased me and said he wanted to ride the tricycle too. This was an amazing special memory.

Retelling the Story of the Gift

This story was told to me so often when I was growing up. As a child living with her older grandparents who had little money, I never owned new toys. Receiving the tricycle in my early years from my uncle meant a lot to me. I am not sure why I attribute such a strong emotion of caring to the tricycle, likely the gift from him resonated with a sense of belonging. On the other hand, it was amazing that I could have this item, deemed a luxury. Possibly this experience stands out because my grandparents could never afford to give me such an item. Tricycles in the community were uncommon largely due to the cost and access to these items. People who could acquire them needed a job and the means to travel into Williams Lake to purchase them. My uncle and aunt were young, and they both worked, and they had no children of their own yet. This might have been why they could gift me with a tricycle. Or perhaps it was because my uncle cared so much for me that he wanted me to be happy.

I could only ride the tricycle in the house or in front of the house on the hard packed roadway because there were no paved streets. When I reflect on this event, it seems amazing that I remember it because I was quite young; however, I recall that my youngest son has a memory from when he was two. He clearly recalled where we stored our lawn mower in a wooden box behind our duplex. He spoke about the lawn mower often and I was amazed. I wonder, now as I inquire into the story, if what I am recollecting is not the actual living of the stories but the stories that I was told about this time.

I grew up learning and understanding that the people surrounding me had a strong sense of caring and sharing. I could hear my grandfather telling a story about how it is important to give the shirt off your back if you had to. He put this into context by suggesting that you consider who needs the item the most. It was part of who we were. An extension of my grandparents' generosity was when they invited expectant mothers from neighbouring villages into their home to be closer to the hospital in Williams Lake for delivery. Their home was not very big and we did not have a lot, yet they extended support to other people. They were able to house the expectant mothers in the attic of our one-room log house. I experienced a strong sense of caring and sharing in this fashion.

Sliding back in time, I do not remember Christmas gift-giving as an important or even a practised event. Yet, as I grew older, I often wondered why I never spent time with my family during Christmas. I remember my grandparents never fussed over Christmas either. There were no Christmas dinners. What I do remember is trying out for the Christmas choir to sing Christmas carols during Christmas Mass, which I never accomplished. I recently discovered through conversation with Elder Jean that Christmas was not our Secwépemc celebration. She explained that the events around Christmas were brought in by the Catholics. This explained why it was not a big event in my memory or a big part of our lives, as I have grown to practice it. I was relieved to learn and realize that Christmas gift-giving was not our way of life because I had felt left out in my earlier years. Now I realize that my grandparents gave me solid, priceless gifts in many other ways. They did the best they could with what they had. My grandparents' lived experiences are associated with the Depression.

Stories from the Landscape of My Early Years

Aside from the tricycle, I also played with small wooden blocks. I pretended they were cars as I pushed them around in piles of dirt, mimicking the sound of the car's motor outside the front window of my grandparents' house. I accepted that I did not own any toys and I was content. I spent hours playing alone with my wooden cars. While I played with them, I recollect that I wore denim coveralls and high-top black canvas runners.

There Was Nothing Flashy about the Way We Lived

Now as I slip backward in time and place, I realize my clothes were more like boy's clothing than girl's clothing. I wonder if my grandparents bought boy's clothes because they were more durable. Without a lot of money, they could not afford frequent new clothes. Or were the clothes given to me by others? Or maybe they were hand sewn? I wonder now how I got my clothes. Perhaps they were durable because they wanted me to be outside or they needed the clothes to last longer. I wonder if it was my grandmother, grandfather, or possibly my uncles who shopped for my clothing. There were no stores on the reserve and the closest stores were in Williams Lake, eleven kilometres from the community. I wonder how my grandparents got into Williams Lake to shop. I remember living in comfort, but there was nothing flashy about how we lived. We had all the necessities, nothing extravagant. I remember feeling slightly uncomfortable being dressed in boys' clothes though. Maybe I stood out from the rest of the children my age. I wondered if it was because my grandparents didn't pay attention to how other children my age were dressed, because girls normally wore dresses. For now, I am grateful that I had everything that I needed as a child and my grandparents took really good care of me.

My Grandpa's Back Pocket

I remember the times I accompanied my grandpa, always behind him hanging on to his back pocket. I was around four and I felt content, somehow knowing I had a good life. My grandpa and I walked to collect water or to visit people around the main village. I was his shadow, walking alongside him with my right hand in the left back pocket of his jeans. The water pump where we gathered water in buckets was not too far from my grandparents' house. In my earlier years, as I hung on to my grandpa's back pocket, we would go to the log house adjacent to the water pump and my grandpa would visit the people there. I accompanied him and stuck by his side, hence the meaning of shadow. We were always attached. I remember another house across the reserve from my grandparents' where they would go for regular visits too. I believe close relatives lived there. I remember feeling really close with my grandpa while I stayed close by his side. Hanging on to his back pocket was normal for me. One memory of this pocket stands out in particular. I envision it being a nice sunny day. As we were walking along, I heard a sudden tearing noise. It was the sound of the pocket tearing off my grandpa's jeans. I remember surprise that I was standing beside my grandpa holding the pocket. I remember I wasn't afraid. My grandpa and I stood still and laughed. It was pretty funny to all of a sudden have my grandpa's pocket in my hand. I am not sure if the pocket was sewn back on the jeans or if a new pair was bought. There was always another pocket to hang on to. This is the most vivid memory of the closeness I had with him.

My Grandparents Are Gifts

The time I held on to my grandpa's pocket was in the early 1960s. I would have been four and my grandpa would have been sixty-two and my grandma sixty-one. Although they were in their senior years, I do not remember them as such. They were quite agile and vibrant. I was never limited in my mobility while I lived with them, and I had been with them from birth. Even though they were retired, I remember the comfort of knowing they were always close by.

I often heard people talk about the hardships and the struggle for food; times were tough in those years. The people were still recovering from the 1930s Depression and the Second World War, which ended in 1945. I heard conversations about food rationing to make sure that everyone was cared for in the community.

I knew we never went hungry; we always had good meals. My grandmother cooked while my grandpa did the physical work of chopping wood and carrying water. As I inquire into this story, I can see my grandmother in the kitchen, starting the fire in the cookstove powered by wood so she could prepare a meal. She got the fire going with dry pitch and thin kindling. The fire would start quickly and heat the stovetop. Remembering the crackling sound of the wood is comforting.

As I slide back in time, I remember our one-room log house. Upon entering the house, the table is in the corner on the left. Beside the table is my grandmother's bed and next to it is my grandfather's bed. A short distance from my grandfather's bed is the bed I slept in. Beside my bed is a cupboard holding dishes. Beside the cupboard is the stairwell leading upstairs to the attic. Next to the stairway is the wooden box that held the firewood to feed the kitchen and potbelly stoves. Beside the wood box are the pots and pans hung along the wall. The kitchen stove is close to the wall to allow for connection to the stovepipe through the ceiling. Next to the kitchen stove is the water bucket and wash basin where we cleaned up. Toward the centre of the room is the potbelly stove used for central heating. Being a child, the house felt spacious; I realize now that it wasn't that big. I wonder where we kept our clothes.

While remembering these earlier landscapes, I wonder if my mom was still at the Coqualeetza hospital as I do not remember seeing her. I cannot recall when she came back to the community and when I saw her again, and I do not remember seeing or being with my dad either.

I was alone with my grandparents. My uncles were adults when I lived with them, so I was the only young child at home. My grandparents had a lot of time and attention to invest in my upbringing. I spent many days with them while I gained my strong work ethic, especially from the way my grandfather taught me. Both my grandparents were gentle people. I cannot remember an incident where I was even scolded. I would say that my childhood was carefree.

Sliding back in time and thinking about the age I would have been when I engaged with my chores, I noticed they were my formative years. What I remember from those days is the good feelings I got from finishing my chores (packing wood and water) and being rewarded. Because certain food was sparse, I remember appreciating the treat of an apple, orange, dried fruit, and occasionally candy. The reward system taught me how to work and earn my treat. Sometimes I asked to do chores to earn my reward. My grandpa would play a game with me before I was rewarded. He would pretend he did not know why I sat next to him on his bed. I sat beside him and waited and, being a child, it felt like a while. He eventually gave me the nod to pull the cardboard box from underneath his bed to find my treat. This is how my grandpa succeeded in his teaching. To this day, I maintain my work ethic both physically and mentally. I hold my grandfather in high esteem for having the patience to teach me.

As I retell the story, I can sense those long-ago feelings of safety and comfort. My grandfather probably felt comfort in knowing that I was beside him too. Until I engaged with narrative inquiry in my study, I avoided thinking about my earlier landscapes. I do not understand what causes me to avoid sliding back to those days even knowing time spent with my grandparents were happier times. Because I can only remember minor glimpses of my childhood, I connected with Elder Jean and my uncle to help locate myself in my earlier years.

Attending School

When I was six, I started school at the Community Day School on the reserve. I was there from Grades 1 to 5. It was a short distance from my grandparents' house. My grandmother walked with me to the top of the hill and watched and waited until she saw me get down to the school doors. I walked the short distance to school every morning and I walked home for lunch. My grandparents prepared my lunches, and they usually ate with me unless they were too hungry to wait. They rose early, especially my grandpa. I recall that he was awake and having his coffee by five o'clock every morning. If my grandmother did not walk with me, she made sure there was another student I could walk with. I was not allowed to walk alone until I was eight. The school was too close to the access road into the community, which fed off busy Highway 97. Highway 97 cut through our community above the school. I remember being in one large classroom with students from primary to intermediate grades on the main floor of the schoolhouse. I think the higher grades were on the basement level of the school. Our desks were lined in straight rows facing the front of the class from which our white teacher lectured. As was common in rural schools at the time, one teacher taught the entire room of students. I remember following strict rules in the school. We had to put our hands up to ask for permission for everything, mainly to use the bathroom during school hours. We could not leave our desk until the teacher gave us permission. Sometimes this was uncomfortable, especially if students had small bladders and drank too much. Possibly I did not experience too extreme levels of anxiety because I knew my grandparents weren't that far away. I recall enjoying school and being a fast learner. I didn't have any trouble with the material taught. I always got my homework done and I rarely was disciplined for not getting my work done. There may have been a few times that I had to stay in school after hours to practice my multiplication tables or my writing skills. I found the multiplication tables difficult when the numbers got higher. My grandparents did not help me with homework much, but they made sure I did my work on my own and they helped me practice reciting the multiplication tables by listening. All my school supplies were provided by the school. Students received a certain number of supplies, which were labelled, and each student was responsible for them. Supplies were replaced as writing books were filled or pencils and erasers wore down. It was difficult to get replacements if the items were lost. There was no library in the school. Textbooks were issued and these were not replaced if they were lost or damaged because the school only had a set amount to hand out. If a student lost their material, they had to borrow from someone.

For Grade 6, I left the on-reserve day school and was bused into Williams Lake daily. I recollect instances during my elementary school years at Marie Sharpe Elementary in Williams Lake that were very uncomfortable. Beyond reach of the teachers, I overheard my people being called "dirty Indians" and the girls called "squaws." Native students were targeted with these names on the playground, in the classrooms, and in the washrooms. The name-calling would come from other students; I do not recall hearing mean words from adults. These words were unusual for me; my grandparents never said them, and we did not own a TV, so I wasn't exposed to these hostile words until I mixed with non-Native students. I did not understand; I knew they were not nice words. I wondered if the words would stop if I washed my skin until it turned white. Having these words thrown at me was painful, and for a while, I wished that I wasn't Native so I could fit in. I told my grandparents about the bad words and their advice was to not pay any mind to what was said; these things were not true. My grandfather reminded me that I am not less than anyone, and his words helped me cope.

I was materially poor living with my grandparents because they were pensioners. I never really felt it until I went into the public school system. Integrating with non-Native students introduced me to competitiveness and status. I did not fit in if I wasn't competitive in sports or if I did not have stylish clothing. In my class photo, I wore canvas shoes without laces, and I was made fun of. Another negative experience I remember was when teams were picked in physical education, I could expect to be one of the last chosen to a team. Other students from my community were treated the same, but I did not become part of a group – I remained a loner. I had often heard the saying, "Sticks and stones can break your bones, but words can never hurt you"; but the truth was, they did. The nasty remarks were painful. I put up a barrier to protect myself from allowing the words to penetrate. A deeply painful memory was when our class prepared to present a play for family and friends at the school. I articulated how I felt in a letter to my mother on June 24, 1990, "The one time that I was really hurt was when I was in my sixth grade. We prepared a concert for our parents to present at the end of the school year. All of my classmates' parents were coming and they asked where my parents were, and I wanted to die." All I could say was, "They are not here." Although I knew my grandparents did not have the means to travel from the village to my school, I felt left out. This was an unprovoked strike on my sense of belonging. I attended Marie Sharpe Elementary for another year to complete Grade 7, then off I went to Williams Lake Junior High School.

My Elementary Experiences in Public School

When I reflect on my integration into the public school system in my elementary years, I remember leaving the comfort and safety of my grandparents' home and community and entering a hostile environment. In my primary years, I experienced the discomfort of having to wait for permission to use the bathroom for an extended time and I had to contain my bladder so I wouldn't mess myself and be thrust into an arena where I felt like a second-class citizen. There was nothing welcoming about my new school. It was larger than my one-room school and there were less people like me. I learned very quickly to keep my thoughts to myself and to metaphorically disappear. On a positive note, my early school landscapes taught me how to be strong and resilient.

The absence of my grandparents from my school community was difficult, but I understood that they did not have the means to interact with the school. On the other hand, it is very likely that they did not feel comfortable going into the public school, so they chose not to. Thinking back to my elementary school days, I do not recall my grandparents being actively engaged with my school even on-reserve. Yet, they had the foresight to influence me about the importance of acquiring an education.

Moving to Residential School

In September 1968, I was moved to the Cariboo Indian Student Residence (formerly St. Joseph's Mission). The school operated from 1868 to 1981. At the time I was placed there, the residence operated as a boarding school and students were bused to the 150 Mile House or Williams Lake public schools. I was twelve when I left the comfort of my grandparents' home; my grandpa was a month away from turning seventy, and my grandma was sixty-nine. They could no longer provide for me. At the residential school, I was placed in the senior girls' dorm with several other students. The large one-room dorm was separated by age group. I was placed among the younger girls. I made a few friends, but I do not recall spending a significant amount of time with anyone in particular. I do remember trying to get a glimpse of my brother on the school grounds or during meals so I could talk with him. I felt lost and missed my grandparents a great deal. There were mainly Secwépemc, Chilcotin, and Carrier students. Many of the Chilcotin and Carrier students could speak their language fluently, and I heard them talk to each other often. I could not speak my language and I did not hear others speaking our language either. I recall the adults who kept watch over the students were referred to as supervisors. When we addressed them, it would be Mr., Miss, or Brother or Sister if they were part of the convent. Many of the laypeople were Irish. If our actions were deemed to be out of line, we were strapped. I remember the supervisors being quite strict. The students were issued chores to complete daily and weekly. The chores were inspected and if the job was not approved, they had to be redone; if at that point they did not pass inspection, the whole job had to be repeated. I stayed at the residence during the school year and returned home for summer breaks. In my final year at the residence, the senior students moved to the fourth floor, and we were assigned to shared rooms with one other person of the same gender. It was more private, and we had closets to store our belongings.

I relied on my ability to excel in school, and I plunged into my schoolwork to stave off the negative feelings I manifested from my public school experiences. Eventually, my hard work paid off. In ninth grade, I was one of six Native students (four from Williams Lake and two from 100 Mile House) selected and sponsored by the Department of Indian Affairs to participate in an all-expenses-paid six-week tour of Europe with our school's social studies program due to my honour roll standing. The trip organizers placed a limit of three hundred dollars on the amount of spending money we could bring. The rationale was to promote fairness, so some students would not have more than others, and to teach students responsibility. The residential school administration took care of all travel costs and the four students from Williams Lake were tasked with raising the spending money. The residential school cook regularly baked a huge supply of doughnuts and several students took turns selling them on the street corners in Williams Lake. I can clearly recall this event. I was shy about selling doughnuts on street corners, but we raised the funds for all four Williams Lake students over several weeks. My grandparents were not involved in my Europe trip. Since I attended the residential school, I saw them only when I went home for summer break. I had no means of communicating with or travelling to visit them.

Reliving Some of My High School Experiences

The anxiety of living with strict rules at the residential school was negated when I was awarded the trip to Europe. Throughout my earlier years, I did not have fancy clothes or trips; my grandparents were only able to provide me with the means to survive. The travel experience to Europe was a life-changing event, opening a new world for me. As a result of this trip, I developed a desire to travel and learn things. I was a young girl, only fourteen years old. I have limited memories of the trip, and I can only recall the names of the countries we travelled to in Western Europe. My experience of living on the fringe during my school years lasted up until Grade 11, and then things began to change. During my senior high school years, Grades 10–12, I attended Columneetza Senior High. I continued to practice my strong work ethic and I kept up my grades. I discovered that I was a fairly strong competitor in high school team sports, and I was no longer overlooked when teams were picked. I began to be selected to a team sooner; I experienced inclusion. I also had teachers who were supportive of my studies and appreciated my gifts.

As I walked about the UBC campus from 2008 to 2014, it felt surreal to be there because I never believed in myself enough to consider an education beyond high school. My confidence grew by remembering my grandfather's advice to never feel less than who I am.

A Story of Moving between the Residential School and My Grandparents' Home

I returned to the residential school around 1976 to live and work. I worked at the Cariboo Indian Student Residence up until it closed in 1981. While there, I was recognized with a jacket bearing the crest shown in Figure 3.3.

I never did wear the jacket. I am not sure why I did not, but I keep it in my treasure chest of memories.

When I worked at the residential school, I drove the five minutes to my community during lunch hours to provide care for my grandparents by cleaning

Figure 3.3 Cariboo Indian Student Residence crest. | Courtesy Georgina Martin

their home. Frequently, on weekends, I took them into Williams Lake and waited for them while they did their grocery shopping. I witnessed my grandpa signing his pension cheque with an X. My grandmother could sign her name. The enjoyment of grocery shopping was how my grandparents demonstrated their independence. I sensed that they enjoyed the trips, and they both appreciated how they could make their own decisions about what to buy. The trips required a lot of patience; they would not be rushed.

Retelling the Story of Caring for My Grandparents as They Aged

I deeply respected my grandparents for taking care of me as a child, so without hesitation, I took the initiative to care for them in different ways. It was not financial; it was by physically helping them. I had my own toddlers to care for at the time. My grandpa was seventy-five and my grandma seventy-four when I made trips to the community during lunch hours to help them out. I understood that they enjoyed the independence of living in their own home and they liked to do their own grocery shopping. To support them, I helped to keep their environment clean. Eventually, home support workers cleaned homes for the elderly and people with physical limitations. On some days, visiting and listening to their stories about their day was sufficient to let them know they were cared for. Since I had a driver's licence and a vehicle, I could drive them in and out of Williams Lake to shop. This was a big event for them to enjoy their independence by physically shopping. Each grandparent would take their own shopping cart, and I would occasionally check their carts, removing items they doubled and tripled up on. I scheduled up to two hours to allow them their freedom to shop. This was their major outing as they had limited mobility. Another event that my grandfather thoroughly enjoyed was attending the Williams Lake Stampede. I drove him to the rodeo and sat with him if I could. If I could not be with him, I made sure he was seated, and I picked him up and drove him back home at the end of the day. He attended the rodeo annually until it was too physically challenging for him to get up and down the stairs.

My College and University Experience

I was a single parent and raising my eldest children when the vision to pursue higher education reappeared. From 1981 to 1983, I took up the Diploma in Business Administration at what was then Cariboo College and is now Thompson Rivers University in Kamloops, BC. Although I consider myself to be a hard worker, my grades were mediocre during that time. In 1983, after I completed my summer internship in 100 Mile House, I decided to work instead of returning to school. I then accepted a position in Prince George, BC, and relocated in 1984. My youngest son was born in 1987 and my youngest daughter in 1990. Unexpectedly, the vision of pursuing an education again returned in 1992, and I embarked on what would be my education journey. I started at the University of Victoria, commuting monthly between Prince George and Victoria for one-week sessions over two years. I enrolled in the Administration of Aboriginal Governments Program and, with additional courses, I concurrently completed the Diploma in Public Sector Management in 1994. This experience was somewhat challenging with young children, and I frequently took them with me to Victoria. I recall a vivid and joyous moment with my children on one of my trips when, during bedtime, my five-year-old son read aloud to me from my university textbook. He would on occasion stumble over big words and we would all have a good belly laugh. I worked and raised my family throughout my pursuit of higher education. The quest for education tugged at me again. In 1994, I started my bachelor's degree with a political science focus at the University of Northern BC (UNBC) in Prince George. I completed my Bachelor of Arts degree in 1998 and continued to the Master of Arts degree in the same year. During this degree, life hurdles obstructed my path, and I could not complete the program within the expected time frame. While I was engaged in my thesis research, my white supervisor found that she could not help me connect with my intention to explore identity from an Aboriginal worldview. It was prudent for me to just get the thesis done. The discipline was also not friendly to writing from the autobiographical "I" position. I did receive a one-time extension and managed to complete the draft of my thesis. A further time extension beyond the draft was denied. I spent the entire 2005 year negotiating my way back into the program to complete the degree. With the support of a Maori scholar, I presented a proposed strategy and outline to graduate studies at UNBC, which was accepted, and I transferred from the political science stream to interdisciplinary studies with a new committee and completed the degree in 2007. I am positive that the resilience and perseverance that carried me through my education journey came from my grandfather's vision for me to get an education. My resilience was articulated by Monty Palmantier, the education director of Lake Babine Nation, during his presentation at UNBC's Indigenous Graduate celebration, when he spoke on my behalf.

May 26, 2007
In essence, Georgina has been consistent in her perseverance and this had been a key ingredient to the success she has attained academically and professionally. The expression of "where there is a will; there is a way" comes to mind. Though Georgina was dealt some roadblocks, even by this institution, in achieving her Master of Arts degree – she persevered! Again in terms of a metaphor, I am reminded of the quality of water (which those fish swim through toward their spring spawning grounds) – water will always find a way; either around, through, or over whatever stands in its path. In that sense I am mindful of the strength of this Secwépemc woman.

Monty's words are a strong example of perseverance. When I struggle and feel defeated, I remember my early landscapes, and the important teachings of my grandparents' work ethic reinvigorates my will to complete tasks, such as the challenges of attaining the master's and PhD degrees.

I moved through a process of telling, retelling, living, and reliving memories of my lived experiences. I recollected the earlier landscapes to the best of my ability. My memories of these landscapes would be more vivid if I had photographs to reflect on. Yet, I am satisfied that the memories of my growing up years with my grandparents are the most comforting. I have figuratively placed the memories of my life with them as the most outstanding. My grandparents gifted me with strong values. They continue to be my tower of strength. I understand that it is up to me to retell my story. I am finally able to acknowledge how a single or several traumatic events affected my outlook. I can remain where I am or decide to move forward. I believe my life has already moved forward on many fronts. I found the strength in myself with the help of my grandparents' voices (blood memory) to attain my university degrees.

I have seen growth in myself throughout my academic journey at UBC, especially in taking up the responsibility to learn how to drum. I moved from experiencing fear about handling my drum to acquiring the confidence to sing and lead the Women's Warrior song solo. I gained the understanding of how to restory my history by also thinking about the rhythm of the drum's beat. The reverberations caused by the stroke of the drumstick as it connects with the drum tell me about how my grandparents took care of me when their daughter was not able to. By reflecting, I understand how my grandparents took up the family and cultural responsibility to raise their daughter's child. With another stroke of the drumstick, I remember how my grandfather loved me, allowing me to be so close to him by hanging on to his back pocket, and how my uncle showed me how much I was treasured when he bought me the tricycle. My grandparents accomplished what they set out to do: raise a healthy and strong individual. Then the drum goes off beat, when memories of rupture and discordance occur as I remember feelings of not belonging during my earlier school landscapes. The cadence is lost, but then the beat becomes strong again as I gained acceptance in school. The drum continues as I learn to be in sync with a view of "Drumming Our Way Home" on many fronts. Messages come to me that show growth in my lived experience and I can rest assured that I have done and continue to do the best that I possibly can. I am sure that this is all my grandparents would wish for.

The drive to do the best I can with what I've got was shown to me by my eldest daughter in my birthday card in 2013. She told me that although my mother was absent, I have been a good mother to four kids. She included a poem she wrote for me in about 2007.

Strength of a Mother
Strength of a mother
Has given me guidance
Strength of a mother
Has given me independence
Strength of a mother
Has given me wisdom
Strength of a mother
Has shown me her integrity
Strength of a mother
Has given me dignity
Strength of a mother
Has shared her knowledge
Strength of a mother
Has shown the warmth of her heart
Strength of a mother
Has shown her leadership
Strength of a mother
Has made me a better daughter
Strength of a mother
Has made a place to call home
Strength of a mother
Has shown endless love
"Strength of a mother"

I gained solace through the words of her poem. Through the retelling and reliving of my stories, I realized that I did enjoy a sense of belonging that I could not recognize until I relived my experiences. I understand that I can retell and restory my lived experience in order to dispel my sense of loss and feel more grateful and positive about my earlier landscapes.

In the next chapters, I write the narratives of Elder Jean, then Colten. I share Elder Jean's and Colten's stories to provide historical and current insights into our cultural identities while emphasizing the importance of Secwépemc people knowing who they are. The intention is to share their stories as teaching stories by presenting the narratives of both Elder Jean and Colten in their own voices. Then I offer an interpretation through Indigenous storywork to enhance the meaning of the lessons in their stories.

CHAPTER 4

Elder Jean's Stories: Passing the Drum Forward to the Next Generation

Elder Jean reflects on Elders' teachings by applying Dr. Archibald's Indigenous storywork model to share back as a give-away for passing on Indigenous Knowledge. This important process invokes heart, mind, body, and spirit.
- JO-ANN ARCHIBALD, 2008, 143

Elder Jean's Story

In this chapter, Elder Jean William shares her lived experiences. Her stories are highly valued teaching stories. She passes along the knowledge and practices of the Secwépemc traditions that she learned from her grandparents. Jean's experiences helped her to look within herself and draw from the positive interactions she had growing up with her grandparents. She inherited the richness of the Secwépemc culture from them. I became a recipient of her teachings and I found that, in many ways, my life story parallels hers in respect to growing up with and learning from grandparents. The power of Jean's stories aligns with Archibald's (2008) storywork approach to make meaning of how the stories are used and the way they are told. Archibald states that stories are significant for "teaching, learning and healing" (2008, 85). The learning begins with excerpts of Jean's stories that she shares in her own words. The story sharing illuminates her feelings and knowledge about Secwépemc identities in a historical and cultural context. The stories begin in Jean's voice and are followed with meaningful context in relationship to Secwépemc identities throughout the chapter.

Jean's Background – Social and Economic Conditions

I was born in 1940 and that's when we travelled with horses, wagon, and horseback. We didn't have vehicles until 1957–58. We never got bored; the kids rode horses a lot. Most of our time was spent with family; we were tight knit. In the fall, we distributed dry meat among families that really needed it. During the winter is when hides were cured. We rarely went into Williams Lake, but when we did, it was a really big event. We cleaned up at the sweat lodge and put on our go-to town clothes. We rode horses alongside the wagon. There were two roads going into Williams Lake on either side of the lake. We went into town one way and came back the other. When we travelled into Williams Lake, it was mainly to get basic supplies like rice, flour, sugar, and syrup. Supplies were rationed back then; we got one can of Rogers syrup. We never bought meat. We would get some of our teas. We got dried wild tea from the meadow too. We had tons of wild tea, roots, berries, and our medicines.

On the way home, we picked berries; sx'usem, saskatoons or choke cherries. It depended on the time of year. Sx'usem was the first berries to pick, then saskatoons and choke cherries. The berries were dried. Toward the end of summer it was t'nis (cranberries) and then crab-apples. When I was a little girl, I used a darning needle to thread the apples together on a string. They were hung out to dry and later stored in gunny sacks.[1]

Jean's reflection illustrates the social and economic conditions in our community following the Great Depression from 1929 to 1939. Grocery store supplies were limited to necessities – rice, flour, sugar, and syrup – and goods were also rationed. Meat was not purchased, which meant that the community relied on the land – hunting and gathering. I sense very strong family cohesion and kinship ties. Kinship is expressed through Jean's experience from the 1940s and I felt it with my grandparents into the early 1960s. Families spent more time together playing and working. Because vehicles were scarce, mobility was limited. Horses and wagons were the most frequent modes of transportation and, of course, it took longer to get to places. Families shared the excitement of travelling into town and Jean describes it as a major event for everyone. The travel served dual purposes. On the return trip, berries were gathered; the berry depended on the season. The people were self-sufficient and caring. The necessary foods were collected for sustenance and all families in need were given provisions. Seasonally, hides were cured for making jackets, gloves, moccasins, and drums. Items could be sold for economic stability, but

Grandparents' Marriage – Making a Life

> I recall my grandfather had an arranged marriage the first time he married. It was in the late 1800s or early 1900s; he was either in his late teens or early twenties. He was promised an inheritance of hay fields and gardens here at Sugar Cane if he married Grace.[2] He married Grace but he didn't get the inheritance so he worked hard to develop his own property. He acquired Wycotte flats and created fields. In his first marriage, he was given a cedar basket. It's a woven basket and I think it is a Carrier basket – my great grandmother was Carrier. It's handmade, unbelievable workmanship. My grandfather tied the basket on his belt and put oats inside it to spread the oats for planting. The basket is from the 1800s and it is weathered. When you look at it, you can see how closely woven it is. I treasure the basket with all my heart, it is one of the most significant things I have. This type of gift was in his first wife's dowry. I have the dowry, or trunk. The dowry was given by the nuns. Back in the day, the girls were fifteen or sixteen when they were married.
>
> When my grandparents were married, it was second marriages for them. Grandma was born September 7, 1895, and Grandpa was born on August 22, 1880. They married in 1934; she was about thirty-nine and he would have been fifty-four. I think my grandma was in her fifties when I lived with them.
>
> My grandparents were a twosome, we called them the lovers because they always hung on to each other and they were close, always at each other's side. They were committed in their marriage.

Very much like me, Jean holds her grandfather in high regard. From Jean's story of how her grandfather toiled to develop property and create fields, I sense that having a strong work ethic is an important quality for our people. My maternal grandparents worked very hard and I inherited the same trait from them as well. I was not aware until my conversation with Jean that dowries were practised among our people. I never heard of this while I was growing up. This does not appear to be part of our cultural practices but was introduced by the nuns.

The Carrier basket signifies long-lasting quality in craftspersonship and sentimental value that cannot be priced in monetary terms. The basket is over two hundred years old, and Jean points to the quality of the artisanship that went into the weaving. The handicraft work and Jean's memories associated with the basket have withstood the test of time.

When Jean mentioned the young age that girls were married – fifteen or sixteen – it made me think about my mom. She was born in 1933 and married in 1949 at the age of sixteen. I am the fifth child of nine; when I was born my mom was twenty-three. Reliving these memories helps me think of my mom's experiences in a different light. Being so young and having many children must have presented some difficult challenges. I think back to how frightening it must have been for her to be quarantined with TB at a very young age. I have no idea when my mom was placed into the Coqualeetza hospital. Because of my sense of loss, I have not yet made the effort to put these facts into perspective. Becoming more aware helps me understand what life must have been like around that time. I wish I could have spent more time with her.

Family

> My grandfather had eight children; four boys and four girls. Your [Georgina's] dad was the youngest. My grandfather lost his first wife when all eight children were quite young. Christine, Aunt Sophie, and your dad were brought up in the convent. Our grandfather worked at St. Joseph's Mission ranch when his children were young.

It seems that our families were quite large; Jean's mom and my dad came from a family of eight and my mom and dad had nine children. There was increased demand placed on parents to support so many children. I learned that my dad was raised by nuns in the convent, and he was motherless at a very young age. This could explain how the absence of affection has permeated our lineage, especially keeping in mind Duran's (2006) explanation that when emotions or trauma are not dealt with in one generation, they are passed on to the next. If my dad was not exposed to affection, then how could he learn how to express affection? My dad was subjected to very damaging circumstances that impaired his development as a child. Through my study, I am learning about these events, which will, of course, help me place my challenges in appropriate context as emotions of resentment are replaced with empathy.

Relationships – Siblings

> My grandmother Geraldine was born during her mother's first marriage, before her mother became a Grouse. Her mother had two more daughters, Eileen

and Diane. These are grandma's half-sisters. In our culture, though, we don't say half-sisters or half-brothers; we are all sisters and brothers. This is important to point out because it shows the family cohesion we practised in our culture. My grandmother's father was Kistemt.

Jean points out a very important aspect of Secwépemc culture in terms of relationships. I understand how brothers and sisters are considered "whole" regardless of the family makeup. I learned that relations extended beyond bloodline. People could be welcomed as brother or sister or aunt or uncle by how they interacted within the family or group. The title was given according to how the person modelled caring and sharing behaviour. While I was growing up, I remember my grandparents being very cordial to visitors, and they were also treated well when they visited in other homes in the village.

Kinship

Grandma Geraldine was married to a chief in Alexandria and she lived with him there. When he passed on, her brothers and sisters brought her back home to Sugar Cane. She had an adopted son with her, Sam, the other son stayed in Alexandria. When she came back after the passing of her husband, it was customary for her to refrain from picking berries while she was in mourning. She could eat fresh salmon and fresh meat in moderation. Because Grandma couldn't pick berries or work with fresh salmon or fresh meat, Tse7emp gave her this basket as a gift when she returned.

I did not know that when my grandmother married my grandfather she inherited eight children. I was confused and I started asking questions when I was about ten. My grandpa said, "I have lots of wives." He was just joking. All my aunts and uncles from Grandpa's first marriage were like grandma's own children, she never called them stepchildren.

Jean explains how various relationships reflect family cohesion. Geraldine was not forgotten when she married and moved away from the community. After her husband died, her family brought her back home from a Carrier community. The children from the marriage were welcome too. When she remarried, she inherited eight children that she raised as her own; they became her children. The close relationships show how accepting people were. Jean mentions the customary ways of the Secwépemc people that were practised when a loved one passed on. There are certain activities that the person who loses a loved one refrains from doing while they are in mourning. This custom is still practised. The intricate details are not for public sharing.

Grandparents Practice Respect

> When we talk about respect, my grandfather highly respected my grandmother. I don't know of anyone else who highly respected their mate. They sat side by side in the wagon and they sat side by side outside their house. They were always together. They didn't only respect each other, they respected the land, the animals, and everything. They needed the horses and cows and the land they owned. They respected the kids. My grandfather really enjoyed them. They would come around and he would sit outside and watch the kids. He never disciplined them or yelled at them. They were all aware that he was there. He would give them a drink of water from the bucket; we never had taps. That was the kind of rearing we had.
>
> I grew up with my grandparents and I feel most privileged that I can speak my language now and I am fortunate that I learned all my traditions. They took me at a very early age, I was probably a baby. I was either two weeks or two months old. This was our cultural practice in the early days when I was born. A child was chosen and raised by grandparents. And when the child grew up, they became responsible for caring for the grandparents in their senior years. I was told my grandparents took care of me when my mother and father went to work. When my mother came back from her employment, my grandparents would not give me back. They said, "We'll keep her and she will be responsible for us in our later years." This practice was well known. I wondered about this in my teens and I carried a lot of pain. I understand it now and I accept the arrangement in a positive way; I embrace it – my grandparents gave me a special gift.

Jean explains her observation of respect, which was practised by her grandfather toward his spouse, grandchildren, the animals, and the land. She also expresses her gratitude for the environment she grew up in. Initially, Jean felt emotional pain as she did not fully understand why she was raised by grandparents. She felt rejected at first until she realized in her teens that grandparents raising grandchildren was a cultural practice of the Secwépemc people. Now she feels privileged for all the values she was taught, especially learning the language. She learned to appreciate living with her grandparents as a gift because she learned traditional ways and she can practice them. Jean's story illustrates the grandparent/grandchild bond and her story helped me feel more grateful about growing up with my grandparents as well. I often wondered about my arrangement, which separated me from my siblings. I concluded that living with my grandparents was a special gift too and I gained a lot of value from their teachings that I might have otherwise missed. I appreciated the insight I gained from Jean for showing me the importance of intergenerational cultural bonds and practices.

Teachings – Respect and Love

> My grandmother took care of my personal grooming. She used the wash basin to get me ready for the day. She braided my hair. I didn't like the way she did it. She would pull my eyes back like a natural face lift. Then she scrubbed my elbows and made sure my fingers were clean from the time I was little. She helped me put on my socks and shoes and she tied my laces. These are the things I remember. She never told me she loved me. I knew when I got up in the morning I could go to her and we never had bad words for each other. In respect to showing affection and showing love, my grandmother was the person in my life that showed me that.
>
> With my boys, I show love and appreciation. I am not afraid to say, "Willie, I love you." Love comes into it, the word is deep. In the past, I would put my head on my grandmother's lap. I loved that. My grandson does too every now and then. I miss it.

An important message I gain from Jean's connection to her grandmother is how love and affection is shared and expressed even without physical contact. Love and connection is shown by the care and attention grandmother extends to granddaughter through personal care. It reminded me of how my grandparents took care of my personal grooming and taught me how to tie my laces as a young child. Until Jean shared her story, I did not realize how much love could be shown without ever saying "I love you." I truly realize that I was loved too. I can feel why the memory of my grandmother singing "You Are My Sunshine" to me carries raw emotion. That was my grandmother's way of showing her love.

Jean understands how important it is to pass on love to her children and grandchildren and she has the ability to openly express it. She acquired the practice through her own experience with her grandparents. The love was there and did not need to be verbalized. I grew up within the same environment. I feel that it is now my responsibility to figure out how to express love more fully.

Lessons about Survival

> They were instrumental in teaching me about survival. I lived in the same log house with my grandparents. My room was upstairs; I had my own little haven. I shared the upstairs with my brother. This is where the dry berries were kept. My grandparents looked after my brother too; he came into the family when he was about five years old. Later, my brother was taken by Aunt Connie to support her because she was a single parent. She lost her husband when her children were really young.

The situation with Jean's brother supports the sharing and caring nature of our people. Her brother was cared for and later sent to an aunt so he could help her care for her children. The Secwépemc had developed a strong stable communal safety net to ensure the survival of families, especially those who needed extra support. I can understand how younger family members were sought out to maintain and protect family cohesion. Jean and I experienced similar situations; we were raised by grandparents and in later years we reciprocated by caring for and supporting them. I understand now how grandparents accepted the responsibility to provide care for their grandchildren and keep them in the community rather than subject them to foster care. I learned that the actions of our grandparents were unselfish acts of love that supported Secwépemc cohesion and the transmittal of cultural practices.

Pictures – Memories of Horses and Wagon

> The picture on the wall here of my grandparents is one that your brother took. I asked him for a copy of it. I don't know when it was taken, I saw it on the wall in his house and I asked for a copy and he shared it with me. I have several pictures of them together. Some really early ones when they were really young, like in their seventies. I guess I'm saying I'm really young, I'm in my seventies. I treasure their pictures. I treasure him with his horse and wagon.
>
> Grandpa used to travel with his horse and wagon. I have pictures of it and I have a picture of your siblings all around our wagon. They would play around our house. He just loved to have his grandkids come around and play around the wagon. I have tape recordings; I can hear the kids playing. Alec and Ivan and all of them, they were really little.
>
> I went for the horses for my grandfather. That was the connection we shared. I would get the horses when he needed them and he would sing to me. I looked after him; if I didn't show up, he would know. Our day started at 6:00 a.m.; I fed and watered the horses then we had breakfast. I always had a horse to ride.

It is clear that Jean had a special reciprocal relationship with her grandfather. Her cherished memories are recollections of photographs and her lived experiences. There is a pattern of activities shared between them, and it sounds like when the pattern was broken, life would feel out of sorts. The horses and wagons were very important as a mode of transportation and a gathering place for Jean and her grandpa and for the other grandchildren. I sense that there were feelings of magic in the relationship and the activities shared between them. Culturally, I feel their kindred spirit.

Secwépemc Practice – Caring for Grandparents

> My grandparents never really explained to me why they took me; I started questioning my mother when I became an adult. She said that she never gave me away, my grandparents wanted me. They knew that when I got older I would be responsible for looking after them, sort of like an old age home where a lot of our people are going now, which is sad. We don't take the time to take care of them like we used to. My grandpa never went to the hospital, he died at home. I looked after him. It was probably one of the best parts of my life, getting to know him and enjoy him. We laughed a lot and spent a lot of interesting times together. I bathed him, cut his hair and his soopjean, cut his toenails and cleaned his ears. I would roll his cigarettes and give him his brandy when he needed it. He never drank much, only when he was under pressure. Later in life, he started to drink brandy before he went to bed. He also loved egg nog with brandy for breakfast. Granny never drank in her life, only tea.

Jean speaks of a very important custom within the Secwépemc culture. The Elders were kept in the community and given the necessary care as they aged. I would say that they lived a dignified and respectful end of life, and there was no alternative; they kept their place in the community. Grandparents took the necessary steps early on to invest in a grandchild's upbringing so they didn't have to worry about who would care for them when they couldn't do things for themselves. The Secwépemc people had a very solid social system in the early years. Jean acknowledges that the system is no longer in place; the elderly are placed in homes and most likely relocated out of the community because the community is not equipped with the appropriate resources to provide the necessary care. Liability is also a major concern nowadays and it is an important consideration regarding care for the elderly. People must have the proper credentials to avoid potential harm or risk to grandparents and the elderly, especially if they require mobility assistance or regular medications.

Like Jean, I am thankful that I was able to provide some care for my grandparents, though the care I was able to provide was limited due to my other family responsibilities. I had a young family to take care of at a very young age. I did the best I could at the time.

Grandmother

> I couldn't look after my grandmother the same. She died of cancer. She had a big growth and she needed morphine. She was hospitalized and I asked the doctor to move her to Vancouver in case she could be saved. She eventually died in the Vancouver hospital. I didn't really like the way they looked after her, but that was the best we could do back then, there is still no cure for cancer.

I sense Jean's heartfelt loss because she could not provide the same level of care for her grandmother due to her major illness, which needed immediate and constant attention. Jean decided that it was best for her to receive care from the medical system to help prolong her life. In this situation, the community could not facilitate at-home care and keep her there. In some situations, it is handy to have options. Unfortunately, I could not take care of my grandparents to the same depth as Jean because I started a family when I was very young. I was respectful to them and I provided transportation and a clean environment for their comfort.

My Grandpa as Advisor

> My grandpa had an advisor role, that's really interesting because that's the kind of role I play now. I call myself the cultural advisor. The hereditary chiefs would come to my grandpa when they experienced problems. He had leadership; the chiefs would go hunting or fishing with him. While they were visiting, the chiefs asked for his input, and his advice would become part of the decision. The chiefs would reach a consensus.
>
> He was respected by his children and by the community. He really took care of us. When he came back from town we knew that he would have a box of popcorn for us. Out of nostalgia, I still buy the same popcorn.

Jean describes how her grandfather played a leadership role in the community. He did not hold a leadership position or chieftainship, yet he was considered a respected advisor. I heard that certain individuals were born with innate leadership qualities and they could be placed in important leadership roles as a result of the way they behaved and carried themselves. Jean's grandpa fit this role. I do not think it is coincidental that Jean finds herself in the role of advisor; she was exposed to leadership throughout her life through her grandfather. I noticed that when her grandpa's advice was sought, the location was never in a boardroom, meeting room, or even in the home, it was on the land while hunting or fishing. I suggest that nature and its surreal surroundings provided spiritual guidance and bore witness to the events.

Sharing Chores

> I was never really disciplined. I wasn't told you got to do this or do that. When there was a sweat lodge, Granny would say, "We have to get the water ready." It was what we did and we didn't question it. When we went to church, the bell would ring and we knew it was time to get ready. We didn't have to be told, they didn't boss us around. Like today it seems like you have to boss people around and tell them when they have to get ready. It was the same when we needed wood, we would get ready and go get it. We learned everything from the time we were little. We helped with everything when we went berry picking; getting the baskets, food, and water ready and loading it up. We knew everything had a place. My grandmother was disciplined in how she put the food together; she would open up the tarp and an apple box or something similar was used. Everything had its place, the knives, forks, spoons, sugar, butter and everything was wrapped. The food went in the wagon and Grandpa looked after the horses. I brought the horses and my grandpa would hook them up and check all the harnesses to make sure there was nothing broken, and he checked the wagon too. He made sure his gun was in a safe place and Granny would look after the knives. We all played a role. We weren't in each other's way. We all did different tasks. In the fields, Grandpa cut the hay and grandma raked, bunched, and cocked the hay. When my grandpa was in his seventies, he often rested. He needed a lot of rest, that's what I am, seventy-one.
>
> Grandpa would say, "Let's pick berries." We all got our baskets ready, put on our hats, socks, and shoes and away we went. When we filled our berry baskets, we came home. Those were the things that I observed.

I can attest to Jean's story about not needing to be disciplined and given orders to do chores. I was raised with the same discipline. During that era, our community worked as a collective and people were attuned to what their tasks were. The adults carried out heavier duties and the children and Elders took care of lighter loads. There was no strict method of how activities were completed; for example, the water levels in the bucket did not have a set standard nor did the woodpile have to be a certain width or height. Everyone contributed to the best of their ability, there was no quality check on the work. People took pride in their effort. Certain cues meant certain activities were under way and the family members took up their post depending on the event. There was no time wasted in organizing, things were accomplished in a timely manner. The work ethic was very strong and calculated. Children gained important work habits at a very young age. Grandparents instituted sound safety practices for all events on the land. I feel the strength and sheer enjoyment in Jean's memories of family gatherings. Families truly appreciated each other. There were fewer outside influences as well. The influx of modern conveniences also played a role in work ethic. Children in the late '60s and early '70s became accustomed to the reduction of manual labour. For example, horses and wagons were no longer prominent in the gathering of wood for the stoves; motorized vehicles and equipment made it quicker and easier. Then electric or propane stoves and central heating systems almost eliminated the need for gathering wood at all.

Jean recalls there were hardly any vehicles in the community, and I too remember that very few families owned televisions or telephones. Radios were the most frequent form of entertainment and communication.

Spirituality

While I was growing up, we always thanked the Creator. We took time to be thankful for what we had, especially our health; my grandparents both had excellent health. Our spirituality was practised on Sundays when we were out on the land. My grandma closed the tent and we said our prayers. It was instilled in us in our youth. My spirituality is very important.

Church was a big part of my grandparents' lives; they went to church every morning and evening and we all attended Mass on Sunday. They were really involved in their spirituality. They never questioned anything about the Catholic Church. Church was a way of life. In my own life, I questioned it because I had a lot of negative feelings; even today I question that part of my beliefs. I know it's not the Catholic Church, it's the people that were in the church, I try not to focus on bad feelings. I am experiencing my own healing so I try to forgive people. That's my own belief; I don't expect anyone to believe what I do, I don't impose my beliefs on others.

I understand that church was a regular congregation where most everyone came together on Sundays. It was time for people to see each other and visit too. I did not feel tension against the church as a young child, but I did fear God from conversations I heard about what happened to people who misbehaved. I was told that people would go to purgatory and spend a long time there, until they offered penance for their behaviour, or they went straight to hell. These places sounded very scary; I did not want to go there. I remember my grandmother attended faithfully too and she led the prayers. I always sat with her toward the front of the church, and I always wore nicer dresses to attend Mass. I heard the service in English and the prayers were in English or Secwepemctsín.

Jean and her grandma recognized the Creator, while my grandmother did not, or not openly, if she did. I suppose everyone had various feelings toward the church, yet it seemed to be a place for weekly gatherings without question.

Familial Relationships

> I call some of the people that I went to residential school with my family; Mary is a sister to me. She is my cousin but I call her sister; we spent a lot of time together at the residential school, she is part of my family unit. I call all of you my nieces and nephews instead of cousins. Your [Georgina's] mom and I were really close in age, we were just like sisters when she married your dad. I remember asking for permission to listen to her sing. She played the guitar and she sang lullabies to the kids. We spent a lot of time together and we used to do crazy things. When the men were out, we would go horseback riding and we acted crazy when we were younger.

As previously mentioned, kinship is not based solely on bloodline. Family cohesion was strengthened and carried stronger ties depending on interrelationships. Jean explains how she considered people she shared residential school experiences with as family. The experiences created strong bonds. Jean extended a caring role toward me and my siblings. She chose to call us nieces or nephews, which is closer than cousins. Familial ties were stronger culturally, no artificial borders were created.

I appreciated hearing Jean speak of my mom's talents. I am learning that she was truly a gifted woman. She was a fun-loving person and a good friend to Jean. I remember her being a hard worker. She took me and my two younger sisters with her once to her workplace; I do not recall the year or our ages, I just remember we were very young. She had a chambermaid job at the

150 Mile House Hotel. We walked there from the community, so we would have been old enough to walk the 4.8 kilometres. As I move through the process of storytelling, I am finding out that I can reach back and bring forward some memories of my mom, and I am fortunate to be an extension of her.

Cultural and Traditional Practices

Over a year ago, this past March, I lost my brother. A lot of people helped me out. Because of his passing, I couldn't pick berries or dry salmon. I really missed that, it is instilled in me. That's something I learned from this basket. I call it the culinary arts basket; it represents the food I am giving away now. I gave Dora some jams because she helped me a lot. She provided food and money for my brother's funeral. She was always there; Thomas and Minnie did the same for me. They are the people I am giving food to, and I learned how to do this from this basket. It is a gift my grandmother got when she lost her husband. Her husband was a chief. The culinary arts basket is fairly large and it could have a layer of dry meat, dry salmon, dried berries, and dried roots. The basket is really beautiful. The concept is about giving. It's a gift; like I gave Dora jarred goods. Traditionally we didn't have jars; the food was put into baskets to give away. I picked up the concept of the culinary arts basket and practised it when I lost my brother. I didn't really have to go to that extent. I cut my hair and I refrained from picking berries or handling fresh salmon and fresh meat. That's how we give instead of using money.

I broke with tradition when my brother died. I went a bit overboard like giving up berry picking and working with fish. Usually the people in really close relationships with the person who passed on stop traditional practices. It would be husband, wife, or child. I wanted to experience that whole concept, so when my brother died I took on this practice. I only wore dark clothing and cut my hair. Then, if I went out into the bush I couldn't stay there for long. I guess it's that we never forget these teachings.

My grandmother picked plants in the spring and made powder for poultices. The poultice is used for colds. She taught us to dry meat and fish, to prepare my own jams, and pick berries. My grandmother couldn't read or write but, man, she could make jams. My son Willie is carrying on these activities now; the tradition has passed down to his generation. My nine-year-old grandson is learning how to bead and sew; he sold a necklace yesterday for twenty dollars. It is important to supplement our income for special things.

I practice my sweats. We used to have sweats at the meadows and a sweat at the river. It was at the Fraser River where we had our fish camp. We called it "Cqwellnekwetkwe," in English it is the Wycotte fishing ground. It's past Chimney Lake or Chimney Ranch on the Fraser River.

I am going back to our great grandmother, old Marie's traditional way of dancing. I dance at Pow Wows. I am looking at how she danced and how her regalia were made. I don't have any pictures so I am working from how it was explained to me. Mavis told me a story about when the older ladies were down by the creek, where the creek and the river meet. They were supposed to be having a sweat but they were dancing. The men were drumming and the women were dancing. She told me how old Marie did her dance and what she had down the front of her dress. I am replicating the scarves with beadwork down the front of my regalia.

I always remember that hard work gets you somewhere. It's not money, it's knowledge. This is what I got out of the training from my grandparents. That training is so valuable. I never get tired. I'm driven by the knowledge that was passed on to me. I thrive on it. I was taught so much; this other stuff is secondary. I am fortunate, I also have the language. It is really important to own our roles as mothers and aunties and to be true to that.

My son is preparing a hide right now. I helped him, we both scraped it; he did most of it. I gave him guidance on what to use and how to scrape the hide. He is carrying on the tradition. My sister Ann and her daughter Heather prepare hides on occasion too. They don't do it very often though because the hides are lots of work.

I learned from my aunts, my grandmother and grandfather, where to find the best saskatoons, and I know where to pick the best cherries. I know where the good fishing spots are, and I know where the animals are out in the territory. I listened to all the stories, and I have an abundance of information.

There were stories shared about coyote. One night, the owls were telling us a story. The way the owl was telling stories some kind of event was going to happen. They would share stories about the duck with babies too. I have a binder of coyote stories; coyote plays an important part in our myths.

Jean continues to practice culture the way she learned it. After losing her brother, she allowed people to take care of her as the community traditionally took care of each other during her growing years. She often mentions in her conversations how people always looked out for others during times of need. This is the Secwépemc way. Jean is living the legacy of her grandparents as she continues to practice and pass on traditions and the important teachings she inherited from them. Jean mentioned something really important that Colten and I have inherited as well; she said we never forget the teachings. This message brings hope that the silence of our traditions can be revived.

Because she is very rich in the culture, she continues the practices in many ways. What she does not know, for example the regalia, she learns so she can work on preserving more knowledge about Secwépemc practices. Jean plays a very important role in passing on cultural practices to her family members and community members who want to learn. I have a strong impression that it is her role as cultural advisor to ensure that the traditions are kept alive. Jean spoke of the sweathouse and I remember going with my grandmother to them as a child. We went to a sweat beside the creek. I recall the steam from the hot rocks were unbearable for me in my youth. I would lie close to the ground and lift the covering so I could breathe in the cold air from the outside, otherwise I felt as if I was going to suffocate. I was too young to understand the spiritual qualities of the sweat for the Secwépemc people. In my adulthood, I learned this, and I practised sweats in my territory with my lifelong friend Lena.

Making Baskets

> A lot of love goes into the baskets; now I make baskets. I started making a coil basket but I didn't finish it yet. It is one of the first baskets I tried to make. I do things in the customary way, the way I was taught. The baskets are made from birchbark and cedar roots. The bigger baskets are for storing the berries and the smaller ones are used for picking berries. I haven't used my gift baskets from Maggie; they are too fragile. I dropped one when I was showing it and it cracked. These are for display only. I usually don't bring out my old baskets, they are too fragile; the one I brought out for you now I normally don't handle. I prefer not to touch them anymore because they deteriorated. They were used for food gathering and you could put hot rocks in them too.

Baskets are very significant items that keep Jean connected to her cultural roots. She shares stories about the intricate detail and craftspersonship in the basket weaving and she further describes how they were used. The stories told are very important because the practice of basket weaving has not flourished nor is its cultural significance known. This part of Secwépemc history could become extinct if the traditions are not passed on or recorded (see Figure 4.1 for a close view of a Secwépemc basket).

90   Drumming Our Way Home

Figure 4.1   Close look at an original Secwépemc basket, from all angles. | Courtesy Georgina Martin

I recall using cedar bark baskets to help with the berry picking as a child. They were very light. The smaller baskets were used for collecting the berries as the larger baskets were filled to capacity. I am not sure if the practice of making cedar bark baskets has thrived. Jean explains how the value and craftspersonship of the basket expresses the love from the basket maker. A lot of care and attention goes into the making, from the gathering of materials to the finished product.

Seasonal Food Gathering

The fall season is when we hunted. The men hunted for moose, deer, ducks, and wild chickens. Our diet was 80 to 90 percent of what I call bush food. Moose and deer meat were dried and we ate chickens. The berries were dried in the summer. We sold our cattle in the fall and that's how we lived from year to year. The winters were long and the cattle, chickens, horses, and dogs had to be fed all winter long. If the winters were severe, the animals had to be fed a lot. In the fall, our firewood was stockpiled for our wood stoves; we had no gas heat. We relied on the bush for everything.

We followed the seasons; we called them seasonal rounds. In the wintertime, lots of stories were told, especially in the evenings while we were at the meadow. We talked about our day and talked about what we saw. It was always interesting when we had visitors. A lot of people like my brothers or my dad or Uncle Tom would come on horseback. They would tell stories about what they saw on the way; the number of ducks, rabbits, moose, deer or anything that they saw on the land. They would tell Grandpa how his children were and how the chief and other people in the community were doing. We never got lonely. We never had a television, only a radio. We listened to the daily message broadcast and the news. This was our means of communicating and finding out what was happening. Telephones were rare so in order to contact people in the area we called into the radio station and had our message sent to whoever we needed to reach through the radio. We knew that our message would get to the person because if they missed the message a family member or friend would pass it on.

For the rest of our food supply, we had about four gardens, two were potatoes and two were vegetables. We had two, maybe three cellars. These were underground; there were no freezers back then. We grew enough potatoes for all of our extended families, our aunts and uncles. The families took a bucket of potatoes, carrots, or turnips whenever they needed it. There was no abuse; we all shared. We shared a lot at community events too. We had full barrels of dried salmon and dried meat and crocks of salted salmon. My aunts made pies and bread. Our granny would tell us to take what we wanted. The whole family were really caring and sharing people.

In the winter, we started the hides again. My grandmother liked to have some spending money so she could buy a new dress or shoes or buy us clothing once in a while. Granny would make herself some new dresses or she made me clothing. When I went to residential school, she made my dresses and underwear and bought shoes.

Through her stories, Jean teaches the importance of food gathering according to the seasons. The community had a very thorough system to ensure that all their food needs were met. The people knew the time of year that hunting and harvesting were to take place to maintain their livelihood. Their efficient system included gardens and storage facilities, both of which were large enough to stockpile food to sustain families throughout the year. The Secwépemc self-managed this system to ensure there was no waste and the people respected the use of supplies. There was no greed.

The people relied on nature for most everything. The wild game and home-grown vegetables made a healthy diet. There were no preservatives or toxic sprays used in the foods taken from the land. I notice that Jean does not identify processed foods as part of the diet. I understand that people in the community were a lot healthier when they relied on traditional foods. Jean reiterates how the tanning of hides was a viable economic entity and currency to access some goods. Tanning hides is hard work, yet it was a regular component of the peoples' seasonal activities. A lot has changed; there are very few people who tan hides now. Self-sufficiency was a huge accomplishment for the Secwépemc people in the era Jean describes. Modern conveniences introduced by outside influence have seriously weakened the traditional practices of the Secwépemc people.

Community Connections

Right after the Williams Lake Stampede, around the beginning of July, we got everything ready and our family went down to the river and we fished for salmon. We caught salmon and dried them for winter supply. Everything we did was family-orientated. We picked berries and this was our means to provide for the family. My father worked with the ranchers so he never had time to fish for my mother's side of the family. My grandparents and a group of us caught fish for them. When one of my uncles went to war, we fished and dried salmon for that family too. People were selected to do this; the rest of us were always ready to help. This was our practice, we made sure we looked after the widows who lost their husbands, and we prepared dried fish for them too.

My grandpa and uncle Gary would be careful not to overfish so my grandmother would not be worked to death. They were respectful and they would always ask her how many fish she could handle that day. I can't imagine fishing all night and preparing the fish all day. If there were other extended family members like Auntie Lillian to help out then the men would bring more fish.

Auntie Lillian helped with the cooking; making bread and bannock and whatever Granny couldn't do. When I got older, I made the bannock by the fire and kept the fires and smoke going. This was my responsibility until the food was prepared; the men were responsible for getting the wood. Then I hung the fish out and learned how to cook. Salmon was a really important part of our food chain.

Later, we moved to the meadows, above the campground by Asahal Lake. It's about a forty-five-minute walk from the community. We camped there for the summer while we cut hay. We worked on the hay early in the morning before it got too hot. This was a family event, to take care of the horses and cattle. When the heat became too unbearable, we picked berries. My grandfather would take us to the berry patch and he would rest. We hunted for moose in the meadows too. Our family stayed at the meadow until the haying was finished.

Within the family unit, all the sons helped out with the hay, horses, and cattle. Grandpa made sure that all his sons and daughters had wood, deer and moose meat. It was really family oriented. They were all good hunters and they were able to get their own game. If your [Georgina's] dad got a moose or deer or the same with Uncle Gord it was shared and everybody benefited. Community sharing was practised. The same with berries. During celebrations, people from Esket travelled over to visit; the berries were cooked along with the salmon. We invited people in and gave them food and made sure they were warm. Those were the respectful ways and it's not being passed on.

My grandparents were really involved; they would go to all the activities in the community. They went to all the dances and they were involved in the church.

Jean describes the strength of community support. While her father worked, her grandfather made sure that seasonal food supplies were provided for the families that her dad would normally provide for. When a family member was physically absent, people in the community were identified to fulfill the family's needs so everyone was looked after. Help was given to widows or anyone that needed extra support. This was the cultural practice.

Another cultural practice was sustainable harvesting. When the men fished, they made sure that they did not overfish for a few reasons. They protected the fish supply because the Secwépemc depended on salmon as a main staple. To ensure that they had access to salmon annually, they caught only what was needed for sustenance and allowed the salmon to restock for the following years. The Secwépemc were very astute about self-monitoring the food chain. The other consideration was for the women and children who gutted and prepared the salmon for preservation. The salmon would be dried or frozen later when appliances were introduced. The men highly respected the amount of labour that went into preparing the fish, so they limited their catch. They would bring more if they knew others in the community could help.

Respect extended to the alignment of duties depending on the person's ability. For example, young Jean looked after the fires to ensure there was enough smoke to keep the flies and bees away from the drying salmon. The flies were especially bad because they would lay multiple eggs on the salmon, which caused them to spoil quickly. Once infected by the flies, the salmon would not be edible, so Jean had a very important role. I think many of us did not realize the importance of our roles when they were less labour intensive.

Jean emphasizes how work-related activities like food gathering and haying were family and community oriented. Families helped each other out and it didn't seem like work; rather, families and community spent more time together. It was more like a social gathering. When I was growing up, I remember how moose and deer meat was shared throughout the community. When the hunters got a moose or deer, the place where the meat could be collected was announced. People were respectful; they only took enough for themselves to ensure everyone had meat. The community-sharing dynamic spread to neighbouring communities. When visitors came in, they were looked after, and they went home with food supplies.

Identities

> The Wycotte name originates from Esket and it was political when a Wycotte tried to overrule something in the community. There was rivalry and the Wycottes were told that they don't have a say in political matters because they were actually from Esket. That's the white man's thinking. We followed the

mother, we were matrilineal. When our grandfather married his first wife, he was told by her parents that if he married her and moved he would get gardens and fields. So he got married and he never got his fields. That's how Wycotte flat came about; he worked hard to get it. He pulled all the trees from the roots and worked the land. He broke his back getting that land so I will not let anybody take it away.

I never heard anything negative in the past two years. For a while it felt like the people were on our case; it's not like that anymore. I remember the disgruntled would say the Wycottes are trying to have a say and they're from Esket. I never took it seriously, I just thought that I was brought up by my grandmother and I go by her standards so they can't dispute anything.

Gift-giving never was a really big thing. My grandmother loved it even if she was brought flowers. She was the happiest person on earth. If she was given a scarf, she treasured it forever. When I gave my grandpa a bag of candy you would think that he won a million bucks. He loved his candies. I don't think he celebrated his birthday ever. Every day was a special day. I saw the affection and I do the same with my family. I give them jams and things not bought from Walmart. I give them something that means something to them. The first drum I ever made I gave away. That's the way I was brought up, that's just the way I am. I do things because it makes me happy and that's how I show real love. That's what I grew up with; it's what I know and what I do.

There was movement among communities; people often migrated if there was intermarriage. This was the case with Jean's grandpa. He came from Esket and there were politics about this move. He was considered to be someone from the outside because he did not originate from Sugar Cane, so efforts were made to exclude the family from any decision making. This practice is deemed to be unusual. It is not considered a social norm of the Secwépemc but is referred to as "white man's thinking." It goes against the principle of communal cohesion. Normally in our community, everyone is welcome regardless of their previous location when they are a contributing community member.

I was happy to hear Jean explain how our people were not materialistic. I often wondered about gift-giving, especially around Christmastime. Jean set the record straight when she said gift-giving was not a Secwépemc practice. The Christmas celebration and gift-giving on December 25 was brought in by the Catholic Church. Jean calls it the Catholics' celebration, it was not significant for the Secwépemc people. Prior to this, the Secwépemc did not need a special occasion to celebrate, rather every day was considered special. I recall hearing my grandparents give thanks for a new day every day. I sense the feeling of winning a million dollars expressed by Jean when people were presented with a gift of any size or shape. My grandparents gave the same response. I frequently noticed that when Elders are given gifts, they will not use the item. They store them for a special occasion or they may never open or even use the item. It seemed that the Elders wanted to preserve the moment eternally.

The celebratory characterization of gifting is reflected in how the Secwépemc thanked the Creator for everything, including the breath of life, on a daily basis. External forces changed this. It became disheartening; Christmas gift-giving is an example. It can cause people to feel excluded if they do not receive gifts, thereby promoting a more commercialized sense of caring.

Stories of Residential School

> I think your [Georgina's] dad was born in 1934; he went to residential school. I don't know how long they were in residential school. I never got the information from Aunty Sophie and Christine. Our grandpa worked at the Mission ranch. I remember the stories; it was really hard for his children to be at the residential school. Grandpa would eat in a separate dining room with the workmen and this was the only time his children would see him. They were segregated. Aunt Christine said he would come in and have meals. If his children were caught talking with Grandpa, they would get punished and be whipped.
>
> Your great grandfather on your mom's side came from Little Shuswap[3] Band and your great grandmother is from Canoe Creek.

Another defining moment in terms of my identity is Jean's confirmation that my dad attended residential school. I was not sure, but I had a strong sensation that he did. The mere fact that he went there explains a lot about my dad. I heard how survivors of residential school left there with broken spirits because they did not have the closeness of parents. It was a very cold place to be raised, especially as it was done by people who never had children of their own. The priests, brothers, and nuns were there only to do their jobs. They enforced segregation by punishing my dad or his siblings for wanting to see their dad. It would have been painful and confusing for them to be in his presence and not be allowed to interact. Of course they would receive negative messages from the experience and internalize them. I can understand how my dad's residential school experiences as a boy affected him because he did not learn how to express love and affection either. The cycle has continued.

Learning by Example

In terms of identity, there are three indicators that I consider part of oral tradition because when these things happened we just knew from experience that certain things needed to be done without being given orders. We knew when we heard someone chopping wood it would be time to get ready to pack it in; when the sound of the dipper scraped the bottom of the bucket it was time to pack water; and when I heard my grandmother making fire it was time to get ready to peel potatoes, carrots, or onions, whatever would be cooked that day.

We didn't have schedules, we just knew what had to be done. Now with my grandson I tell him to be home by 4:30 because he has chores to do and then I name off the chores. We just knew if Grandpa chopped wood we packed it in, nobody told us we had to. When we heard the dipper scraping the bottom of the water bucket, we knew it was time to pack water; we never had to be told we just did it. It was a modelling kind of behaviour. When cooking was started I knew I had to peel potatoes; this was the kind of respect we had for one another. We knew this well and we learned well. I felt so proud when I packed water in the two-pound pail, then I graduated to the three-pound pail, then I went up to the five-pound pail and then the ten-pound syrup pail.

The relationship that my grandmother had with me from infancy into my adulthood is the kind of respect we had for one another. I knew how she did things. We were a very busy family and we were very productive. In my teens, I remember my grandmother telling me about how the old people lived. Nowadays people are just trying to learn in their teens.

In the recent past, our people needed permission to leave the reserve. I heard the chiefs talk about how the peoples' boundaries should be respected. Boundaries are not respected today. I think that is why we are creating our own problems, because we allow others to more or less come in and dictate to us how to do things. If you look at the band office it works like the old Indian Agent in a sense.

The teaching and learning style has changed drastically from earlier years to now. Jean and I both learned to attend to chores by knowing what needed to be done without being told. We both willingly did our chores for the sheer joy of receiving appreciation. We knew our grandparents were happy when we did the work and that was all we needed to feel good about it. Young people behave differently nowadays. There appears to be a lack of motivation or possibly too many stimuli from technology and modernization.

Our chores were necessary for the family to have drinking water and warmth. Now, water is available by turning on the tap and heat by turning up the thermostat. Modern conveniences decreased the reliance on manual labour but there are still chores that need to be done, especially to maintain a clean and safe environment.

Jean emphasizes how we were taught as well. She mentions that the teaching was role modelled. We learned to respond to the cues when chores needed to be done rather than being given direct orders. I believe we both did so out of respect, to demonstrate to our grandparents how much we cared for them. I am not suggesting that youth do not care for their grandparents now, only that the work ethic has changed drastically from when Jean and I grew up.

The Teachings and Knowledge Gained from Jean's Stories

Elder Jean reflected on her life experiences in her community to articulate her connection to Secwépemc culture and traditions. She emphasized her experiences growing up with grandparents. Her memories are vividly contained in the stories she told, and they underscore how Jean developed her cultural and Traditional Knowledge. From interviewing Jean, then narrating her stories, I learned more about the ways of our Secwépemc people in the T'exelc community too. The stories are special because the oral teachings we receive are not found in textbooks. The stories depict the independence and resourcefulness of the Secwépemc people. It is important to know that the Secwépemc had solid traditional practices that were passed on from generation to generation. The teachings are still being passed along, but to a lesser degree. By listening to Jean describe our cultural history, I am able to affirm my identity and recognize the solid teachings I received from my grandparents.

Jean described how various external forces affected the traditional ways of the Secwépemc people and these influences diminished the strength of our cultural identities. From this learning experience, I suggest that Jean and I are privileged to have the solid lived experiences that connected us to our identities. Jean recommends that everyone take the initiative to learn the culture and traditions before they are gone. By gathering Jean's stories and interpreting their meaning, I found that the stories' meaning helped me better understand myself and my situation (where I came from). I believe retelling and reliving these stories helped both Jean and I understand how we see ourselves in our lives and cultural narratives. The continued sharing of the stories and cultural experiences in the community can help others make meaning of their identities and, in all likelihood, many more people have solid memories of the teachings from grandparents and Elders. Jean's stories about living and learning from her grandparents prove that our Elders did shape our cultural identities and that cultural practices maintained the strength and unity of our people. The transmission of cultural knowledge through the passing on of stories supports the revival and survival of cultural identities and helps us sustain who we are. The traditional lived experiences Jean shares are important to help us achieve the interrelatedness and synergy introduced by Archibald. To understand our holistic genealogy and harmony within our cultural identities requires personal responsibility to learn about traditions and pass on the teachings. Our nation is well positioned to regain our cultural integrity with Knowledge Keepers like Jean in our midst.

This chapter has shared the voice and lived experiences of an Elder; in the next chapter, we hear a youth's voice. In contributing his stories to my intergenerational study about cultural identities, Colten provides insights into how youth today view identities.

CHAPTER 5

Colten's Stories: Memories and Values

I hope young Indigenous readers and non-Indigenous readers both feel like the world is theirs, to go out and make the most of it; that they all have gifts and that they should go show the world what those gifts are. Live a life of positivity.

• WAB KINEW, WINDSPEAKER.COM, JANUARY 10, 2023

Meeting Colten

My first meeting with Colten took place on August 10, 2011. We met at his grandparents' home in the T'exelc community. My gratitude was expressed by providing Colten with food and a monetary gift. Prior to the visit, I requested that Colten bring an important photograph to our meeting. Colten said he thought about bringing a photograph of himself with his best friend and his grandpa on a hunting trip. He described the scene of his photo; the group are sitting inside the box of a red pickup truck posing with a deer. The picture was taken outside Colten's mom's house. Colten explained that the picture is important to him because it brings back memories of times when there were no worries. He recalls and describes his memories throughout our conversations. As with Elder Jean's stories, I first present Colten's stories in his own voice and then make meaning of his stories in relation to Secwépemc identities, which I share in my own voice. The stories are transcribed into text primarily verbatim in the way Colten shared them; I refrained from editing his stories other than to ensure the stories flowed nicely.

Memories

> I am ten or eleven in the hunting photograph. It was quite a long time ago; I was a kid. I miss those days, we did whatever and my grandpa would take us hunting or fishing. I really liked those times. The photo reminds me of when I was worry free. My friend lives in Williams Lake now; he has a girlfriend and a kid. We still hang out once in a while and visit. He fished with me last year where I worked. I was a catch runner down at Rudy Johnson Bridge and he would come down and hang out and fish.[1]

A significant memory for Colten while he was growing up is spending time with his grandpa and his best friend. It was a time of comfort, no worries. He describes how he was exposed to the Secwépemcs' cultural practices of hunting and fishing at a very young age. The fishing activities are important events; he also spent time fishing with his friend. Colten's experience occurred around 2000, which shows that youth today were still actively involved in cultural practices. Colten did not disclose whether youth are still engaged in traditions; he only spoke about his own experiences. Colten practised culture and he developed strong relationships with his family and friends while he was growing up. Throughout my conversations with Colten, I noticed how important these relationships were to him. I found this unique; I do not hear many youth speak about relationships with family in the same tone. Other youth could have the same feelings; I just have not heard it verbalized before.

Spending Time between Two Families

> When I lived with my mom in Campbell River I was in preschool. I was around four or five, I was pretty young. We stayed with my younger brother's dad and his family for some time. Later on we moved to Victoria and we lived there for about a year and a half. I think I was in Grade 5. It felt weird going to school in Victoria. There were a lot of different people around and there were no Natives. I am usually around Natives. There were just streets and I had to watch where I was going and what I was doing. I couldn't just go outside and play and do whatever I wanted like I did around the reserve. I found some friends and it was OK, but I missed home, I guess. I wanted to move back to Williams Lake. It's alright to go away sometimes and try something new and different. It felt like a lot of moving around. Every holiday or something I went with one family and hung out, then I came back.

> We lived in Victoria for about a year and a half; after half a year I wanted to move back to Williams Lake. I did move to Nemaiah and I went to school in Nemaiah for about three years. I finished Grade 7 in Nemaiah and Grades 8 to 12 in Williams Lake.
>
> In earlier years, before I became a teenager, I spent a year with each of my parents on their reserves (Nemaiah and Sugar Cane). I alternated and I spent my holidays between the two communities. I had weekend visits between the two places too, until I was around ten. It was alright for me growing up. When I was with one parent I missed the other one though and I kept switching schools. It wasn't that bad, I knew both communities.
>
> I have not seen my dad for a while now; I have not been out to Nemaiah in a long time. At least two months. That is a long time for me. It feels like a long time because I haven't seen my family. It depends on what I'm doing, I might spend a weekend there, or during Christmas break, I will spend a couple weeks there.

During his childhood, Colten noticed how much he moved around. The moving did not affect him too much because he was able to spend enough time with each parents' families. Colten had developed a strong attachment to both communities. He felt a noticeable difference between living on the reserve and in a non-Aboriginal community. When he lived off-reserve, he felt that there were no others around like him; at least he could not identify them if there were. There may well have been other Indigenous people around who did not self-identify as Indigenous. While he lived off-reserve, Colten did not like the limitations on his movements. This is likely because when he is on-reserve, he feels more secure with fewer barriers and safety concerns. It is noticeably different for him because there are always responsible adults close by to keep an eye on the children; the adults would notice if anything was out of sorts with the young ones and would respond. Adults watching over children is a common practice in many Indigenous communities; a sort of social safety net. I suggest that the feelings of safety are what made Colten's childhood worry free. Colten did miss his family sometimes; he spoke often about missing his dad. I sense that he became a strong individual because of the necessity of balancing his life between two families – a situation that would require a great deal of courage and resilience. He always seemed to keep his emotions in check because he knew he would spend his time between two homes.

The movement of Indigenous youth between families and communities is not uncommon. As Colten explains, he shifted between both. A child or children can be quite mobile throughout the school year when their parents separate or if they have responsibilities in different communities. It is important for teachers to understand the impacts the separation has on the student, which often results in frequent movement between families and schools. The move can be challenging for the student's attention, retention, and overall performance. Their academic and emotional health can be compromised if they do not receive appropriate support in schools. Parents may be reluctant to disclose their personal life situations for fear that the information would generate negative consequences, such as the stereotyping that accompanies single parent status. These feelings of apprehension deny the student's enjoyment of a well-rounded learning experience.

Familial Relationships

> What I make a connection to is my family. They really help me out a lot and they are always there for me. Family and friends are the people I talk to and ask for guidance.
>
> My dad and I sometimes have a real good talk; he helps me out a lot. He's been through a lot in his life and he knows what I'm going through. I really talk to him because he sits down with me and he listens. The family helps me to be OK.
>
> I have four brothers and two sisters. My brothers and sister on my dad's side I haven't seen very much because I haven't been out to Nemaiah. My brother on my mom's side moved back to Campbell River so I don't see him much, and my other brother is a little guy. My little brother stays here at my grandma's and I see him every once in a while when I visit. My sister lives here too. I feel that I don't see them as much as I should.
>
> I never knew my grandpa on my dad's side; he passed away. He is from Toosey. The funeral was last year. My dad and his dad weren't really close. We went out to Toosey for the funeral and my dad introduced me to all our cousins and aunties from out there. I never really saw them before. It was pretty good. We talked a bit and ate supper and took pictures with them. It was a one-time meeting. Toosey is on the way to Alexis Creek just past Sheep Creek Bridge. It is about twenty minutes from Williams Lake. People fish around the bridge too. Farewell Canyon is on the other side of Toosey.

Colten shows in his dialogue that family is very important to him and he recognizes that he does not see them enough. Although he spends less time with his family, he feels highly supported by them and knows they will help him through situations. He knows they are there for him in times of need. It is exciting to see that Colten has his family for support. Unfortunately, there are many people who grew up without strong supportive relationships. I noticed his relationships were nurtured during his growing years.

Colten shows that his familial relationships are his strength. Although he did not have a relationship with one of his grandparents, it does not seem to affect him. He had a one-time connection and seemed to have accepted it. Given that many Indigenous people suffered from the effects of residential school, it is promising that there is positive growth in familial relationships.

Life in Nemaiah

> It is a three-hour drive from Williams Lake to Nemaiah. The roads are better now so it can take two and a half hours to get there. There are lots of travellers from many parts of the world that visit Nemaiah.
>
> During school, our Chilcotin classes went on field trips. The youth worker brought us to sweats, fishing, hiking, and berry picking. We visited the Elders and watched them tan hides or smoke fish. The Elders taught us to pick berries, make bows and arrows, and things like that. There was cultural week for all the Chilcotin elementary schools. The students gathered at one school and we had lots of activities for a week. There was traditional stuff like tanning hides and making bows and arrows, gaff hooks, and fishing stuff. We did this at the end of the year. It was fun.
>
> I was going to try and fast out in Nemaiah. My dad said when I was becoming a man I was to go into the mountain by myself and fast, but I was scared to go by myself so I didn't go. I was to go for a week and survive on a bit of dry meat and water. I would pray and wait to see something. I thought that was pretty cool because they said whatever I saw or dream about, that's my power.

Nemaiah is not as secluded as it once was. The roads in and out of the community are more accessible and the travel time is shorter. While Colten lived and went to school in Nemaiah, he had more exposure to cultural practices in school and learning from Elders. It is impressive that the schools supported cultural learning by dedicating time for students' exposure to hands-on cultural learning. Culture- and land-based pedagogies are significant approaches to learning for Indigenous students, especially youth, because their learning is more effective when it is done together with their peers. Colten spoke many times throughout his conversations to the importance of spending time with friends and others his age.

Colten was immersed in many of the same activities that Jean describes as Secwépemc practices. He was also able to participate in regular cultural events in his dad's community. Colten was exposed to two distinct cultures while he was growing up, and this experience of navigating and learning within two cultures at the same time was both a strength and a challenge. While the cultural practices (sweats, hunting, fishing, berry picking, and tanning hides) between his two home communities were very similar, there were some differences, requiring him to make some adjustment to switch between cultural teachings. These experiences helped Colten build his strong character.

Although Colten did not practise the traditional coming-of-age ceremony, he is aware that it exists and understands how it works. He knows that, in his culture, to become a man he had to spend time on the land in solitude; unfortunately, he was too afraid. He would have gained power through his dreams. Maybe when Colten is stronger, he can return to the teaching and do something similar.

Community and Collective Stories

> About the community, I see people go hunting or I hear about it when they go fishing. There are some sweathouses around here [Sugar Cane] people go to. I haven't been to a sweat for a long time.
>
> When I was younger, I remember events like the Yuwipi ceremony or a ceremony at the lake, camping and sweats. Mexican people visited our community and they did a full moon ceremony. My auntie knew about the ceremony. It was hosted at the band office in Nemaiah. It was a big ceremony where people stood in a circle. They hummed, prayed, sang, and danced with the lights off. It would be total darkness, everything was blacked out and we could hear an eagle flying around like spirits. They were spirits of old. I heard it was real. I heard things and you could feel it. It was the praying, singing, and drumming that made it happen. Then we passed around a peace pipe. I did it once. It hasn't been done lately, I hear of it in other places, people talk about the Yuwipi ceremony but not around here [Sugar Cane]. I think they still have Pow Wows here. I don't really go to Pow Wows and stuff like that.
>
> Good stories are about power, like healing people that are sick. There is talk about people and bad medicine. People say stuff like your spirit ran away from you. My grandma said one of my cousins was really sick and they brought her to her sister Marjory and Marjory saw this thing running around, it was her spirit. The spirits have different animal names. My auntie and the other girls put hands on you and they feel things. Sometimes they stay in Kamloops

and they have dreams about things that happen over here. They would warn us about what they see in their dreams. Another is the crane, when it made a really ugly noise something bad would happen. I saw a crane a couple times when I was hunting with my grandpa Homer. We were walking around the field just past 150 Mile House in the cut blocks.

I heard stories from the Shuswap and Chilcotin that one day the white man will depend on us. The technology will be gone. They will be learning from us. We will revert back to the old days like living off the land. I heard stories that something will happen in the future that will cause this.

Colten speaks of ceremonial experiences that are not part of either Shuswap or Chilcotin cultures. The ceremony took place in his community of Nemaiah. He had the ability to relate to these events, and he shared how he felt and what he heard during the ceremony. I feel that Colten described spiritual connections that adults may think youth would not understand or relate too. He was connected to spirituality in both his communities. He speaks later on of his grandmother teaching him about signs from the owl and his grandpa teaching him about messages from cranes.

Both the Yuwipi ceremony and Pow Wows are practices that are external to Colten's cultures. I suggest that if Colten was not rooted in his own culture and background, the foreign experiences could have confused him; however, he clearly explains the ceremony as an entity outside of his own practice. He demonstrates in his narrative that he has the ability to separate his communal cultural teachings from others. The ability to do this shows strength in Colten's character because a young person can be negatively influenced or confused by different beliefs.

Colten was introduced to various stories. He says some stories are good and some not so good. The good stories have healing power, and the bad stories cause sickness or separation from your spirit. Stories can appear in dreams, and the spirits have animal names, or they can be associated with birds (he mentions owls and cranes). I believe that Colten is rich in knowledge about traditional ways because of his upbringing. The knowledge he acquired is not available to or practised by all youth. The absence of cultural knowledge can impact a person's ability to develop a strong sense of who they are because culture is an integral part of personal identity, as Colten has described.

Language

I didn't really learn any of the languages. When I was really young, I used to speak Chilcotin, that's all I spoke. I think I moved to Sugar Cane for a while then I lost it and started speaking English. I was really young, I think I was three or four or something. I was just a little kid. It would have been alright if I kept speaking it. I barely know any Shuswap; I don't speak it fluently. The Elders around the Rez spoke it but I never really learned it. I did in school; I took Shuswap classes, but I found Chilcotin was easier to remember because it has shorter words and easier to say, I guess. I never really learned anything about either language. It's hard to answer the question about who I am. If you're not practising your traditional ways you lose touch with it and become like everyone else.

The people fish with a dip net here and I think it's for Aboriginal people unless they have some kind of permit. Sheep Creek is fifteen minutes west of Williams Lake toward Anaham. It's just before Farewell Canyon. On your way out to Anaham or Stony, it's the first bridge going downhill. It's not the bridge before Alexis Creek. This one is not even ten minutes from Williams Lake.

Colten spoke his Chilcotin language fluently at a very young age. He lost his ability to speak Chilcotin when he moved to his other parent's community. Only English was spoken among youth at Sugar Cane, which shows that Shuswap is not spoken fluently in our community. He did take Shuswap classes in school and determined that Shuswap was more difficult to learn and speak. At the time of our meeting, he was not speaking either language. I believe that when Colten is ready to learn the language again, he will not have too much difficulty because he was exposed to it at a very young age. I expect that when I become acquainted with the Secwépemc language, I will be able to learn it without too much difficulty for the same reason.

Although Colten mentioned a few times in our conversations that he didn't know what to say about who he is, he did have some profound messages. Several of his stories connect him to his traditional practices between his two cultures. He acknowledged that because he is not practising the traditional ways, he may lose touch with the culture and he runs the risk of becoming like everyone else. He has a strong value base of how culture connects people to their identities, communities, and families. I believe that Colten has a lot of cultural knowledge and he solidly represents a youth's perspective. He has a lot to teach.

Colten seems unsure about the details surrounding dip-net fishing; I confirmed that the Secwépemc people do fish for salmon with dip nets. Permits were not required when I accompanied fishermen to the river to dip net, but permits are required now. Previously, the Secwépemcs' subsistence was unencumbered. The people took only what they needed to survive for the year;

Sports

> I remember when I was around twelve my dad took me to Redstone for steer riding school. We were learning how to steer ride and I jumped on my first steer and I got hurt real bad, so I quit right there and I wanted to go home. I was in hockey right from the starting level around five years old up until I was in Grade 8 or 9. Then in about Grade 10, I was too old for the minor league. If I wanted to keep playing hockey, I would have to go in the recreation league. I didn't want to do that so I stopped playing. I play ball hockey now. Our ball hockey team plays in Skeetchestn or Seabird and sometimes Lillooet. I used to play baseball but our team isn't active.
>
> My dad owns horses and cows. When I was in my early teens, I used to ride horses all the time. I remember one year I got hurt on the horse so I stopped riding altogether. I kept getting hurt riding horses; I stopped liking them. My dad kept trying to get me back into riding. He would say maybe the saddle was too small; we'll get you a bigger saddle. I just gave up. He still does a lot of horseback riding.
>
> I remember the gymkhana. It is a bunch of games and different types of races. It was fun. I never did it myself because I don't like horses. My dad likes it, he likes horses. Every year at the rodeo in Nemaiah they have the suicide race. It's part of the rodeo. I don't care for it. Beside the rodeo grounds there is a creek and a mountain goes up about a quarter of the way up. The horses and riders go up there and wait. They race down this really narrow trail only one person can get through at a time. There might be a beaver dam in the creek and the water is deep. My dad wiped out a few times. Nobody gets hurt too bad. I think my dad went down once and broke his collarbone.

Colten was very active in steer riding, horseback riding, and hockey in his earlier years. He was introduced to activities that his dad was either good at or involved with a lot, such as horseback riding and rodeos. Colten's dad was involved with livestock, so Colten was around animals a lot too. He was very active, and I noticed how he made decisions and stuck to them at a very young age. When he determined that steer riding and horseback riding caused him injury, he quit, and he would not go back to the activity with any amount of coaxing for fear that he would get hurt again. He particularly did not care for rugged events like the suicide race, likely because of the potential for injury.

Colten shows character in his confidence to make his own decisions, particularly around events that can cause harm.

Learning Experiences – High School Landscapes

One summer, I joined the chief and council shadow in Nemaiah. I shadowed my dad, he was the chief. We went to meetings and events in Vancouver and other communities. It was fun. I tried to take notes, but I never got into it, it was too much talking. I liked hanging out with my dad a lot that summer. I thought it would be cool to be a chief. I wouldn't know what to do.

I would rather go to school for something I want to do. I like working outside with animals. I am interested in marine biology that studies creatures in the ocean or maybe archaeology. I liked science but I didn't really like my teacher. I tried to take physics and chemistry but I couldn't get into it. I tried chemistry but there was a lot of math and formulas I had to take. It was algebra. Biology wasn't that bad, it was just that my teacher was strict in class and I wasn't comfortable. There were lots of people that I didn't talk to so I dropped out. That would be in Grade 11. I was falling behind so I got out of it and took the easier science course, the basic science. I wanted to graduate, so I picked the easy classes so I would actually graduate that year. If I go back, I want to do it soon, the sooner the better. I just need to get started. I think I have to upgrade for a year and take courses like math and science over again because I took the easier courses.

When I went to school, it felt like I had to be there, it wasn't really that exciting. I think I only had summer classes once because I failed. It took me a week and a half to pass. I never spoke to my mom and dad about it much because they always told me to get the hard work done now and it will be easier later. I think in Grade 12 it was mainly my friends that kept me going to school; I wanted to see them every day. It was fun; everybody spread out and moved away.

In school, I wasn't really bothered by racism. There was just one person but it didn't really bother me though. Everyone had my back, I guess, when this person picked on me, it wasn't really racist. I don't know why he picked on me; it wasn't that big of a deal. It didn't bother me and he didn't do it all the time, I guess. He would try and poke fun at me in front of his friends.

I don't really know what to talk about. School was alright, when I was getting close to finishing it was hard because my friends would want to skip out and just do whatever downtown and I would fall behind in class. I would get in trouble with my parents, and, I think, last year in Grade 12, with a month or two months to go, I was taken off the graduating list. That forced me to pull up my socks and get my work done so I could pass. I graduated from Williams Lake Secondary. The school goes to Grade 12 now. I didn't find it really challenging, there was always someone to help me there, like the First Nations support workers. We were really good friends with them and hung out with them all the time. The support workers were really cool. We talked to them when we saw them in the hallway or sometimes they brought us out for lunch or we would have projects in school and they would take us downtown to get supplies. They would take us out of class. It was pretty cool; I found it helpful and comfortable. They tried to help us in any way they could with what we needed. They were older people. They would take us aside and help us. School just felt like something I had to do. I kind of really didn't like school. I had to go there every day and do the same thing and learn for six hours. But it wasn't that bad.

When I was in school there would be some kind of thing down here (Boitanio Park), I think it was Aboriginal Day. I don't do anything regularly on Aboriginal Day. I only attend things I know about.

I really like computers. One time, I was going to take this computer program for three years. I went to Kamloops and talked with a counsellor about the program. As time went on, I didn't feel interested in it anymore. I was scared and it felt too hard to go back to school again after being away for such a long time. I was away for three years going on four.

I kind of see my uncles and aunties like friends or buddies. I don't ask them for advice, I can't explain it.

What we are talking about is helping me reflect on my early years up until now, what I did and who means what to me; it's helping me to be who I am, in a way. I think about who I am from this person, I usually just live my life and I never really thought about it before. I don't really know how to see who a person is really. I'm having a hard time; I don't know what to say. I'm not really the type of person that wants to go and do stuff.

Based on how Colten describes his time with his dad, I detect that relationships are really important for him. While Colten was a chief and council shadow, he was fortunate to receive mentorship from his dad. He enjoyed the time he spent with him; it was an experience and opportunity. Colten benefited from his experience, but it is rare for youth to have this type of opportunity due to time constraints for the mentor and the additional costs of travel. It was likely more cost-effective for Colten because of the relationship. It is an example of how a community invests in their future development by training their youth for leadership.

Colten shares his concerns about school. As a teenager, he had difficulty sorting out what he wanted to do for a career, but he did know that he liked science. Unfortunately, he had difficulty with a teacher, which is not abnormal; maybe the experience could have been managed better if he had a way to develop a response to the negativity. I understand that many Indigenous students can be caught in similar situations because of misunderstandings between teacher and student; these could be due to cultural or age differences. I relate to Colten's story about taking easier courses, I did the same in high school because it felt like the norm. Guidance counsellors directed me to take the nonacademic courses because they were easier. I took business-related courses that only required general math and I avoided algebra and sciences because I was led to believe that I did not have the capacity to complete this level of work. In listening to Colten's story, I realize how things have not changed; he was given the same options in his high school experience. My four children received similar advice when they attended high school between the years of 1985 and 2007. They were directed into the lower-level nonacademic stream, and as a concerned parent, I objected and revised their course loads. Unlike many Indigenous youth advocates who may not have the ability to or understand how to challenge the public school systems on their child's behalf, I was able to support my children. If Colten made different decisions rather than accept the advice he received, he could have avoided the need to upgrade. Decisions to move into nonacademic programming in high schools essentially create the prerequisite to upgrade for college or university in later years. This could be a deterrent for youth to pursue higher education.

Colten speaks of experiences that I heard about often from my teenage children but could not really relate to at the time. Colten helped me understand that many youth feel the same in high school. He speaks of going to school to be with his friends – that was his motivation. It seems that for many youth in high school the social contact becomes their priority. Colten admits that his grades fell because he skipped classes and went off with his friends. He went along with this until he was removed from the graduating class list and he realized he might not graduate. He was reluctant to share this information with his parents, and I sense that this was because of the respect he held for them or because he didn't want to feel he had let them down. He felt more comfortable confiding with the First Nations support workers in the school. Colten's experience reveals how youth can benefit from positive support and encouragement. The role of the First Nations support workers in public schools is pivotal. They provide mentorship and support for the Indigenous students in a caring way. These support workers have a positive impact and they helped Colten pull through.

Colten mentions another important factor about youth and their interests. Initially, he was keenly interested in pursuing a computer program, but as time passed, he developed anxiety about returning to further studies. It is important for educators to recognize this element of fear when they develop strategies to support youth who are considering college or postsecondary education. I suggest that it is vital for educators to understand youth and assist them to overcome their fears; to encourage them to recognize their potential and succeed in academic curriculum.

Losing Interest

> I don't hunt and fish much now; I kind of lost interest. Over time I wanted to hang out with my friends. This would be more into my teenage years, like thirteen or fourteen [*Colten is in his twenties now*]. I can't do things where there are lots of people, I feel uncomfortable. I like to be by myself and do my own thing. I have a handful of friends that I hang out with, my best friend and his brother and some other boys in our age group.
>
> I don't do much now; I hang out with my friends. We play video games or skateboard around town. I don't think I did any canoeing or any sort of activities really.

Colten admits his interests and priorities changed in his teenage years. He preferred to spend more time with his friends rather than hunting and fishing. Fortunately, he developed the cultural practice of subsistence earlier on; when these are learned at an early age, I understand they are never forgotten. I am reminded of this because I anticipate that when I begin to learn the language, I will catch on quickly because I grew up with my grandparents speaking our language fluently. Perhaps Colten will hunt and fish again later on in life.

He spends time with a few friends, and he can also be on his own and feel comfortable. I see this as another character trait Colten developed; I believe that youth can perceive time spent alone as a sign of inadequacy, with people thinking they do not have friends or are unpopular. At this delicate stage in their lives, youth tend to be very vulnerable to other peoples' perceptions of them. I remember being very much a loner in high school, but I made it through. This could be another motivator for why I did well; I think I buried myself in my schoolwork to avoid the loneliness.

Colten's interests shifted more when he was in high school and again into his twenties. His friends became his priority and his preferred activities changed. Like many youths now, their time is spent playing video games and skateboarding. When I wrote my MA thesis in 2007, I mentioned this shift as a threat to our traditional ways; many youths choose to turn away from them and become consumed by technology and modernization. In Colten's situation, he has the knowledge of subsistence hunting and fishing. It is an aspect of his embodied experience that he could easily return to if and when he chooses.

Work Experiences

The place where I work is Rudy Johnson Bridge. People dip-net fish there too. Mainly people from Sugar Cane fish there or they go to Farewell. The Soda Creek people go there sometimes but they usually go to their own fishing areas near Soda Creek by the heritage site. I have never been fishing down that way.

I like outdoor work. I don't think I could sit in an office or behind a desk or any place for very long. I like to be outside and move around and see interesting things. I like animals, I really like animals. I like being outside exploring. I go for a walk up the hill and see what's on the other side. When we go to the river, we wander around a lot and check out what we can find. I am a catch monitor down at Sheep Creek. I monitor the fishermen that are down there and count how much fish they catch and I take a scale sample for each of the fish. I don't really know what the scale sample is for; they didn't really tell us. It could be to tell their age or where they have been. They have this whole big system; I guess it's to see how many fish come up the river and where they are coming from. That's pretty much it.

Through his recent job as a fish catch monitor, Colten learned the Secwépemc people have different fishing areas. Although he wasn't fully aware of the reason for taking samples of the fish scale, I believe his activities are affiliated with the preservation of fish stocks. Colten may not fully appreciate that he was engaged in a very important role to ensure food security for the Secwépemc people. The level of fishing is monitored to ensure that the yearly salmon run is maintained. Excessive fishing depletes the salmon stock and threatens the peoples' livelihood, therefore, monitoring reduces the risk of overfishing. Colten enjoys the outdoors, and his work practices are culturally connected to the teachings he gained from his grandparents. He often demonstrates the knowledge of traditional fishing practices, which is a significant example of the place-based knowledge he learned from family experiences.

Grandmothers' Teachings

> I don't go out to Nemaiah and visit much lately. My grandma, Betty, on my dad's side lives out there. She does different things like feed the cows and prepares hides. When I was in Nemaiah, my grandma would teach us a lot of stuff and we would hang out with her. She would be doing hides, picking berries, or drying fish. In Sugar Cane, I would be with my grandpa hunting, fishing, or drying fish. Sometimes we would pick berries, but mostly hunting and fishing.
>
> Sometimes I see my grandma and aunties when they come into town to do their shopping or when they are on their way to visit family in Kamloops. My cousins are in Kamloops; they either go to school or just live there.
>
> I hung out with my grandma and learned from her whenever she does traditional stuff. She cuts fish and meat for drying. She also tans hides; she would scrape it and let it soak in water for a while. I would help her sometimes; I usually watch because I don't know what to do. That would be my grandma Betty. She always had these sayings, like she closes the window curtains every night because if an owl came and looked at you in the window something bad would happen or if the owl whistled at you at night, it was bad to whistle at night. It was bad for us to whistle at night because something might whistle back at you and you would get really sick.
>
> My other grandma, April, she was always there for me, helping me out, I really love her. She's always worrying about me and giving me advice and telling me not to be bad or stuff like that. Like when I drink or something, she's the one that really makes me think about it. She just makes me think about things. She really helps me a lot and gives me advice and she helps me any way she can. She's always happy and so nice.

Colten speaks fondly of his relationships with his grandmothers and the teachings he received from them while he was growing up. He was engaged in several traditional practices throughout his life, and he refers to them as learning opportunities. Earlier, he said he does not practice cultural activities anymore; but, like Jean and me, the teachings are embedded in his memory. From the conversations I had with Colten, I recognized the high degree of respect that he has for the grandparents he had relationships with. He describes time spent with his Nemaiah grandma as "hanging out" with her. He uses the same reference for his close friends and the First Nations support workers. I find his reference to "hanging out" with his grandma significant because he places his relationship with her in the same sphere of importance as his friends.

I find that youth tend to separate their relationships with grandparents and parents in a hierarchical relationship. By "hanging out," Colten treats his grandma like one of his friends.

It is heartening to hear Colten say he loves his maternal grandma. I do not often hear young people his age openly express love. In my experience, it seems difficult for youth to express affection. He shows gratitude for the advice he receives from her, and he is not afraid to admit that he needs positive guidance to keep him on track. I see this as character strength because Colten is not afraid to accept that he needs good advice when he behaves inappropriately.

Identities

> I am the oldest child in the family. My oldest brother is sixteen. My brother Kyle and my other brother on my dad's side, Sam, he's in Grade 11 now. I am really bad with birthdays; I don't remember them all. On my dad's side, Shayna is six. She's my sister on my dad's side and on my mom's side I have Cindy.
>
> I was raised by my grandparents and my mom and dad. When I was younger, I remember spending time with my grandma on weekends when my dad was at meetings and my mom was going to school.

Colten has siblings from both his parents. He does not remember their birthdays but I do believe that he cares a great deal about all of them. He grew up with his maternal grandparents; they were involved in his upbringing along with his parents. This arrangement contributed to the strength in Colten's character.

> Lately I stay around town because it's easier to get a job and more of my friends are here. I don't hang out with anyone in Nemaiah around my age. They party and they are crazy sometimes. I try not to party but sometimes I get into trouble too. I skateboard with my friends around town, anywhere we can really. Sometimes we are told to go somewhere else, but not too often. We just do our own thing and hang out. It's just usually me and my friend Tony. Sometimes one of our other buddies will meet up with us. We might see him wandering around or see him at the skate park or something. We skate until we get tired, I guess, then we find something else to do or we go back to our buddy Cameron's place and relax, play some video games. We mainly play shooting games; we connect with others. Everyone is addicted to Xbox. That's the main technology, and the cellphone, I guess. We talk to people on the computer. I talk to my friends by computer or text. About technology, most people use it a lot. I think

there are so many new gadgets and different systems. I don't think older family members really use that kind of stuff. My dad uses it and my mom does. I talk to them sometimes.

As Colten grew up, his interests changed. He resided closer to Williams Lake for easier access to jobs and to be close to his friends. He didn't get into the social scene too much. He preferred to hang out with a few friends and skateboard, which is what many youth in his age group were doing at the time. Skateboarding and video games became an important part of youth culture in Colten's generation. He places emphasis on Xbox as an "addiction" because youth are drawn to computers, cellphones, and other gadgets. In his view, many people his age use these items, unlike adults. He knows youth are consumed by technology and they tend to spend more time talking through the computer or cellphones than in person. This trend toward impersonal conversation can potentially impair the development of social skills for teens and there is the risk of negative attacks through social media. Technology has created intense challenges for youth, parents, and schools.

I don't really like talking a lot unless I really need to. I think about what's going on around me and I keep it to myself. Once in a while I did public presentations in school but I didn't like it. The first time I did was when I was in Victoria. There was a whole bunch of kids that I didn't know. I hung out with a couple of them and I had to do this project that I didn't do. I think I had a month to do it and I barely did anything. I never really thought that it was important for marks. I just got up and I said I had nothing and the teacher said OK then I sat back down. But then in high school it wasn't as bad. I knew I had to get it over with.

I conclude that although Colten is quiet, he is a very strong individual. He shows character as he describes a school experience that could have resulted in a negative consequence, but it did not seem to devastate him. He did not complete an assigned public speaking project because he felt that it wasn't that important. Colten did not elaborate on the outcome. It leaves one to ponder what happened; it appears that it must not have impacted his overall grade otherwise he would have mentioned it. Given the way I was taught, there would have been a serious consequence for failing to complete a project and the teacher likely would have made some reference to it in front of the class. The way Colten describes the event, the presentation did not occur and that was the end of it.

> In Williams Lake there wasn't a really particular hangout spot. It didn't matter; a group of us would just go anywhere and do anything or just walk around at lunchtime or grab something to eat somewhere. Someone would suggest something and we would do it. We would wander around and joke around. I think there were about twenty of us that hung out all the time. Not all at once, it would be different groups of people. Like at random places like Walmart, the mall, gas stations, or restaurants.

Colten's description of how he spent his time in and around Williams Lake awoke memories in me of when I attended high school in Williams Lake. The patterns are similar, although I had few friends and our options of places to hang out were less varied. During Colten's era, there were more restaurants, a mall, and other establishments like Walmart. During the late 1960s and early 1970s in Williams Lake there were no big box stores or malls and only a few restaurants. When I was in Grade 11, our hangout was one particular restaurant on the main street in the downtown core. We spent hours sitting in the restaurant usually sharing whatever someone in our group could afford. We basically sat in the diner while we shared the food and listened to the twenty-five-cent jukebox. This was the extent of our entertainment.

We did not have access to sporting events or activities like skateboarding. Technology was not introduced at this point. Stimuli through technology increased in Colten's school experiences. I feel the same nostalgia for high school experiences though. Like Colten, I did not feel a lot of stress. My job was to go to school, and I was content doing as I was expected. Thinking back to my elementary and high school days, although I was not involved in sports, I did not feel deprived, these were just things we could not do, and we accepted it.

> I can't believe I forgot my picture again. I remembered it; I took a picture of the picture with my cellphone. It was sitting right there. The other thing is my car. I feel better when I have a car. Without it, I had to catch a ride everywhere or I was stuck. I use it all the time. I had speeding tickets. I got a speeding ticket and a ticket for a no "N" sign at the same time. So I got a letter in the mail saying my licence was suspended. I got it back, lucky my grandpa was there because the fines had to be paid and he said, "Well I got it, I guess." I signed papers and they gave me a temporary paper until my picture ID came. They gave a date when I could go in and reinstate my licence; mine was September 6, so I went a few days after because I didn't get paid until then.
>
> It was the first thing I bought when I got my money. My grandma had a car and she put insurance on it when I got my licence back. She found it too

hard with only two vehicles because my cousin Leslie has a little family and she needs to use my grandma's SUV all the time. So my grandma and my xpé7e [grandfather] bought a new car for my grandma, my grandma has three vehicles now. She said I couldn't handle it with only two so I had to buy another one. Everyone depends on people with a licence; everyone needs a ride to run errands. Every time my aunty or uncle or somebody needs a ride, they ask me to bring them somewhere or they need to go shopping. I say, "Yeah, for sure, it's no big deal." Sometimes it gets pretty hectic when everyone is doing everything at the same time. I get stressed out and I feel like I am being rushed. It was getting that way before I lost my licence so it was a nice break for a couple weeks. The young people nowadays make plans to drink and stuff.

An important aspect of Colten's life is having his driver's licence, both for mobility and to support his family and friends with transportation. He still carries on with his caring spirit in a conventional way. Everyone needs transportation to acquire goods or attend appointments. For a period when he did not have access to a vehicle, he felt stuck. The independence he feels is important. He admits that the demand feels hectic occasionally, and it was nice to have a short rest from being a driver. I sense Colten's need for a driver's licence is a major priority for him. It is the one thing he can't live without; it supports his independence.

Values Drawn from Colten's Stories

I feel extremely privileged to have had the opportunity to hear and share Colten's stories of his embodied relational experiences. Many times, his stories helped me return to my own experiences growing up in Sugar Cane and Williams Lake. His high school experiences, especially, brought me back to the times I attended the same school. I was reminded of similar difficulties in school settings, which shows that some things have not changed. In addition to reconnecting to life in school, Colten helped me improve my understanding of what youth experience in schools and at home. His stories are invaluable for parents and educators as he reveals how youth interact with family, friends, and mentors. Colten provides insight for parents and teachers to understand youth experiences. There is an opportunity to enhance adult and youth relationships in many areas.

He demonstrates the importance of learning languages, culture, and traditions, which are a major connection to identities. He maintained a strong allegiance to his families as he grew up. The lessons learned from his parents and grandparents are invaluable, as these teachings can only be acquired through healthy relationships with family and community. Familial and cultural bonds are important components of both the Secwépemc and Chilcotin cultures that Colten grew up within. Throughout the conversations, Colten expresses sincere gratitude for the support his friends, mentors, and family gave to him to help him throughout life.

Although some differences exist between his Secwépemc and Chilcotin cultures, they are more similar than different. The two cultures strengthened Colten's knowledge: he did not feel confused. I noticed throughout his story that Colten could separate traditional practices between the two by describing what he learned in each community. Given that he was very young, he could have combined them into one for ease, but instead, he respected them individually. This is a strong indicator of knowing oneself. In his story, he acknowledges how the languages presented some challenges. For Colten, the Shuswap language was more difficult than Chilcotin.

I was extremely encouraged by the strength of Colten's connection to his families and communities. He demonstrates the care he felt for his supports (parents and grandparents) and he expresses love for them effortlessly. His ability to show affection is crucial; it is an example of how youth have developed the capacity to reduce the intergenerational effects of residential school. His character exhibits generational growth, given that Jean and I continue to harbour feelings of numbness and long-lasting detachment from our emotions. Colten's experiences exemplify giant leaps in the personal growth of our people; there is hope for the future healing of our families.

Colten's experience further reaffirms the important role that grandparents hold in passing on important traditions and culture. Like me and Jean, he was exposed to Secwépemc culture and traditions at a very young age. He may have recently separated from his culture, but I do believe he will never forget the teachings that are embedded in his being. Although several times Colten would stop and say, "I don't know how to talk about who I am," he did present invaluable information about youth experiences. During one of our meetings, he mentioned how participating in my study was helping him to recognize who he is. To learn from and support youth, it is essential that adults listen to and learn from them. My gathering of stories shows that youth have a lot of rich knowledge to share.

In the following chapter, I begin with the final conversation, held on December 6, 2011, which brought Jean, Colten, and me together as a collective.

I wished to consider our collective or communal identities because our relationality is equally important as our individual identities. In my analysis of our conversation, I consider the elements of our individual identities that bring us together as Secwépemc people.

CHAPTER 6

Intergenerational Knowledge Transmission

Each of us needs to belong, not just to one person but to a family, friends, a group, and a culture.
- JEAN VANIER, *BECOMING HUMAN*, 1998, 35

BRINGING OUR STORIES TOGETHER

In this concluding chapter, our collective thoughts focused on the stories manifested among Elder Jean, Colten, and I while we celebrated the imparting of our knowledges about Secwépemc culture and identities. Our collective stories point to the importance of knowing that our cultural connectedness is not solely individual efforts; the Secwépemc have a collective history. The quote from Jean Vanier (1998) that opens this chapter draws attention to the need for belonging to our families, our friends, and to our Secwépemc Nation and our Secwépemc culture. Our collective conversation took place at Elder Jean's home on December 6, 2011, where the three of us engaged in a fulsome conversation about what it means to be Secwépemc. We brought our personal perspectives, memories, and experiences to draw on as we reflected on these questions:

1. How do Elders shape cultural identity?
2. How is cultural identity important for Secwépemc people?
3. How do stories convey our cultural identities?

Elder Jean recounted the strong traditional practices that were passed on to her from her Elders and grandparents. Through the teachings, she learned how to pass on the traditions to keep the Secwépemc culture alive. Colten strongly emphasized his familial ties, his connection to two distinct cultures, and the strength of kinship. I remained inherently connected to my culture and homeland through the embodied teachings and memories of my grandparents. These conversations signify how our Indigenous Knowledges were passed down through our stories, the teachings from our Elders and grandparents,[1] and lived experiences. Archibald (2008) describes how, in the Stó:lō tradition, the basket maker gives away their first basket. The sharing of our lives is our giveaway. We hope that these stories encapsulate the power and importance of the giveaway.

Sharing Identity Stories as a Collective

Elder Jean taught us that within our territory's rocks are markers that assist our people to recognize and identify significant places. An example is the red rock called PellTsko'ten found in the Williams Lake First Nation community beside the train tracks; Elder Jean affirmed that this type of rock is used for making pipes. She told us that when you see PellTsko'ten in the territory, you know you are home. This coincides with the lesson she shared in Chapter 1 when she said, "You are not Secwépemc unless you return to the land"; Secwep means both unfolding and spreading out and coming home (personal communication, February 10, 2011). Elder Jean indicated that place names were used a lot in Creation stories. Accordingly, the Secwépemc know the territory surrounding Sugar Cane is our home and the people used these areas for their traditional practices. Therefore, geographic indicators are significant to the cultural identity of the Secwépemc people.[2]

Earlier in life, Jean moved away from the community to attend school; yet, she always knew she had a home to return to. The connection to her grandparents eventually drew her home. Jean recounted a favourite memory when Christmas activities occurred in the community. She would ride on a horse-drawn sleigh with her xpé7e. The horses' harnesses had brass collars and coloured chimes. The families gathered and travelled by horse-drawn wagons into Williams Lake on Christmas Eve to buy a turkey. On the way into town, the travellers stopped at the Point (a landmark pullout beside a jutting rock face) and had lunch around the campfire. Tea, bannock, dry meat, and dry fish were served. After lunch, the party continued their journey. On the return trip, the travellers used lamps to light their way through the darkness. The people in the community saw the lamps approaching and gave the four-gun salute as the sleighs and horses arrived. Everyone was happy when they heard the bells chime. The turkey was prepared for midnight dinner on December 24. The meal consisted of turkey, cake, a bit of bannock, and coffee, or tea; it did not include potatoes, gravy, and all the trimmings like it does now. The people did not set up and decorate Christmas trees; only poinsettias were displayed. Jean said, "We have our own beliefs, and we try to keep our traditions alive in my family." Her story offers a vision of the sleigh ride and the family and community cohesion that occurred around the horse and sleigh event. I understand the kinship that Jean describes as a strong element of our Secwépemc cultural identity too.

Colten fondly remembers his hunting trips with his xpé7e. He observed that he never shot the animals himself. Hunting took place when families needed meat. Colten knew the hunters would prepare and leave the community at five o'clock in the morning the day after hearing that a family or families were in need. Colten tried to help his xpé7e pack the meat out of the bush to the vehicle, but it was too heavy for him, so he carried the gun instead. Children were given manageable tasks, and carrying the gun and taking safety precautions is an important part of learning. Colten practised safety by removing the shell clip from the gun and keeping the gun pointed away from the people. He remembers sawing the animal's bones with a handsaw to hang the meat. He says, "I was a kid so I couldn't help that much." However, during the hunting trips, Colten participated in the cultural practice of sustenance.

He reminds us that his methods of helping others evolved when he got his driver's licence. He borrowed his grandpa's car to give people rides – his grandpa told him to be careful and to drive slowly in the wintertime. Jean acknowledges the value of this teaching for Colten's safety and that of his passengers because the roads become quite treacherous in the wintertime. Colten consistently acknowledges how his grandparents were there for him. His story reaffirms kinship by pointing to the way community support is offered in times of need for food and the family cohesion he has with his grandparents.

I noted that we collectively have strong relationships and connections with our grandparents. Grandparents are solid representations of familial and communal unity for the Secwépemc people. They are the pillars in the community. All three of us had (or still have) grandparents who practised and passed on the cultural teachings and were always present. I assert that the sharing of culture sustained our sense of belonging. Through the sharing of stories, I came to realize that the feelings and teachings I received from my grandparents are gifts. As Elders, our grandparents did indeed shape our cultural identities. I did not fully comprehend how important my grandparents were in my life until I restoried my experiences alongside Jean's and Colten's. The support and teachings I received from my grandparents are what gave me the strength to propel forward. My grandparents went to the spirit world, but their memories keep me connected to my homeland where I was raised. Therefore, I consider the antler handle of my Hand Drum to represent my grandparents. I will always hang on to them. In this sense, I am Secwépemc, and I have returned to the land. I know I am from T'exelc and this is where I belong. Through the collective sharing of stories between us, I discovered the significance of how the stories and teachings we acquired from our grandparents kept us anchored to our Secwépemc beginnings. Despite the toil and disruption we all faced from the assault of external influences in our lives, we remain resilient and connected to our cultural identities through the revered teachings of our grandparents and esteemed Elders. We have survived and resisted.

Revering What It Means to Be Secwépemc

During this journey, I privileged the defining characteristics and importance of Secwépemc identities through stories and literature written by Secwépemc scholars (Billy 2009; Ignace 2008; Michel 2012). I found there are no standard definitions of what it means to be Secwépemc. The meaning or degree of identity is dependent on the individual, according to their embodied and relational experiences.

I agree with Ignace (2008) that the knowledge of our Elders is crucial and we must honour their pivotal role in shaping our cultural identities in Secwépemc society. Ignace recalls how the Elders were ill-treated by the Department of Indian Affairs, who went against their wishes in the past. The Elders set out to defend the Secwépemc territory against the intrusion of outsiders and to protect the right to self-govern our Secwépemc Nations. Ignace (2008) points out that in spite of the Elders' efforts, Indian Affairs instead separated the Secwépemc Nation into seventeen smaller communities and placed them on Indian reserve land that accounted for a mere 1 percent of their 150,000 square kilometres of traditional homeland. Like many Indigenous Nations in Canada and other parts of the world, the Secwépemc suffered from the forced loss of economy, culture, language, and territory in spite of the Elders' efforts to protect them. Ismael Abu-Saad (2006, 1087) offers a present-day example of the ill-treatment of Indigenous Peoples when he describes how Palestinians remain "separate from the Jews socially, politically, and administratively" as a result of government policies that enforce segregation. These colonized projects of nation-states progressed at the expense of the colonized peoples. Ignace (2008) notes that according to the Elders, the Secwépemc people thrived despite interference; therefore, it is vital for our survival that we continue to pass on the traditions and keep them alive. He affirms that the Elders shaped Secwépemc cultural identities through their positions in our society. Ignace (2008, 37) adds, "Our elders not only detail the travels on our land and the use of our resources; their stories ... [as] shared are memories, they are the collective historical consciousness among Secwépemc elders." Secwépemc scholar Kathy Michel (2012, 167) reaffirms the position of Elders: "Not only did the involvement of the Elders provide language to the program, but it also restored them to their natural role in the community as knowledge carriers." Both Ignace and Michel note how the Elders held vital societal roles in the preservation of Secwépemc Knowledge.

It was the influx of European settlement within the territories of the Secwépemc that seriously eroded the traditional ways of life and shattered our systems. Contact threatened and distorted Secwépemc Knowledge and identities.[3] Secwépemc scholar Janice R. Billy (2009) summarizes how the historical fur trade caused massive change to the Secwépemc way of life and how the mixing of cultures affected the beliefs, customs, and values of Secwépemc society. She records how the competitive nature of the fur trade caused fractures in the social structures and changes in family structure; for example, because the men spent more time trapping and less time hunting and fishing. The fur trade modified the Secwépemc economic system because, after the beaver were trapped to almost extinction, the Secwépemc had to trade salmon. This substitution of furs for salmon threatened the food supply. Billy (2009, 53) focuses on the reclamation of Secwépemc Knowledge and consciousness-raising of the people through a decolonization process: "Both of these [consciousness-raising and decolonization processes] are critical to cultural survival of the Secwépemc." She identifies other events of destruction such as colossal epidemics, the arrival of missionaries, and the Gold Rush, which caused further catastrophic damage to the Secwépemc way of life. These events have changed the landscape of Secwépemc identities and must be considered and understood in our efforts to realize their impacts. I believe that people must recognize what they had, and how culture changed, to sort out how to get it back. The documented knowledge of Secwépemc scholars (Billy 2009; Ignace 2008; Michel 2012) is very recent, pointing to the absence of Secwépemc stories and knowledge by Secwépemc scholars in the literature.

By offering the stories of three generations of T'exelc people, *Drumming Our Way Home* makes an important contribution from a Secwépemc scholar that pushes the boundaries and raises critical consciousness about Secwépemc identities.

I echo the strength and endurance of the Elders as Keepers of our Traditional Knowledge. In my journey, the teachings of my grandparents were reaffirmed (honoured), and I have come to understand how they formed my heritage and inner strength. If I had not spent time with them, I would not be able to speak about cultural identity. Elder Jean and Colten acknowledge their grandparents for the same reason.

Based on Ignace's (2008) historical account and my lived experience, I believe one of the most damaging attacks on identities has been the denial of practices that transmit culture. The history of cultural loss is bred by colonial policies and programs, namely the Indian Act, the residential school program, Indian hospitals, Indian day schools, and the resultant enforced denial of languages and culture among Indigenous communities across Canada. James Frideres (2008, 336) states that Aboriginal identity is about "reclaiming suppressed culture." Therefore, for the Secwépemc people to thrive, it is necessary to learn about and own their identities. Unfortunately, Canada's Indian Act still dictates who we are; while the Secwépemc people include kinship and familial relationships as esteemed markers of identity, the state does not. I learned this as a child, and I remain connected to my homeland in my own way. Secwépemc kinship kept the Secwépemc people together in sharing and caring relationships. Kinship is what bound the nation.

The threat to our culture is felt and experienced by all three generations of Secwépemc in my study. I feel connected in certain instances, but I must learn and practice the traditions more. I am currently learning to drum and speak the language. I can drum and sing the Women's Warrior song; I now need to learn how to sing a Secwépemc song, and I must continue to learn the language. I am consciously aware of what I need to do. Meanwhile, Elder Jean continues to practice and pass on the traditions in the most effective ways she can. I heard her say that "it is up to the people, young and old, to take up their responsibility to learn about our culture" (personal communication, August 10, 2011). I sense her concern that the youth have rapidly lost interest, and it is difficult to coach them into the traditional mode of learning. For example, Jean and I learned by listening and observing cues when work needed to be done, while youth today are accustomed to being given instructions or orders. However, Colten has shared the rich cultural experiences between Chilcotin and Secwépemc that he learned growing up too. In his late teens, he separated from his involvement with culture and became more involved with the everyday activities of his peers, namely skateboarding and technology. I believe that, like me, Colten is grounded in his cultures, and he will get back to it when he is ready. My study assisted me to unravel my own identity losses within an intergenerational context by collecting and enquiring into identity stories alongside Jean and Colten.

I consider my contribution of the retelling of life stories through the lenses of three Secwépemc people an opportunity to question why the Secwépemc people have lacked voice and agency in and around the City of Williams Lake. Furniss (1999) raised awareness about the historical atrocities of colonialism, racism, and residential schools in her book *The Burden of History: Colonialism and the Frontier Myth in a Rural Canadian Community*. By moving away from the accounts that have been shaped by colonialism, our stories provide firsthand and genuine accounts of lives lived. As Michel (2012, 254) proclaimed, the Secwépemc "are finding ways to assert their independence and distinct identity." These written stories help us, and others, align with and strengthen our identities.

I barely touched the surface of another layer of racism that's part of my story: the assault on Secwépemc identity instigated by the legacy of Indian hospitals. The back cover of Meijer Drees's 2013 book, *Healing Histories: Stories from Canada's Indian Hospitals,* states that the book is "the first detailed collection of Aboriginal perspectives on the history of tuberculosis in Canada's indigenous communities and on the federal government's Indian Health Services." In her book, *They Called Me Number One: Secrets and Survival at an Indian Residential School*, Bev Sellars (2013, 23) shares vivid memories of when she was admitted to the Coqualeetza Indian Hospital in 1960, and mourns, "I had lost my whole family." I too allowed myself to become more aware of Indian hospitals as I spoke about my own experience of being born in one. A critical examination of the intergenerational impacts of Indian hospitals on Indigenous people in British Columbia must be carried out in relation to family and community disruptions, poor educational outcomes, and continuing health issues. I did not go further than to acknowledge the existence of these hospitals: there is no information in the limited literature available about the effects of these hospitals on the Secwépemc people in my community. What I am aware of is that I was born there. Now, as I reflect on it, I am even more thankful that my grandparents took me from the Coqualeetza Indian Hospital. If they hadn't, I could have been given to another family or adopted out by social services. If either of these scenarios had occurred, I would have been even further removed from my cultural identities.

Our stories show the depth of our inherent cultural knowledge. We know that our Secwépemc identities are rooted in our culture and that culture can be practiced or observed. I suggest that knowing one's identity is heart work. Cultural identity is essential for our continued survival as a distinct Secwépemc Nation. We acknowledge that culture keeps us connected and rooted to our homeland and community. The three of us spoke about our attachment to grandparents and our Secwépemc traditional practices such as hunting, fishing, sweats, gathering, hide tanning, and preserving. Family inclusion and contact with the land are paramount. The sense of connection to family, culture, and community stands out throughout the generations.

Restoring Balance through Hand Drumming

Our lives are embedded in our belief system behind the being, doing, and thinking, which is our Secwépemc Knowledge. While I deepened my understanding, I learned more about applying protocols that protected me on my journey to reveal and speak about my lived experiences. At the outset, I could not anticipate how difficult the retelling of my story would be. Therefore, it was necessary to utilize the appropriate tools to make meaning of both Indigenous Knowledge and the connection to my Hand Drum. I situated and refined who I am in relation to my culture and my homeland, and as my story unfolded, I depicted the importance of identity through discovering who I am. This is important to fulfilling my role as an Indigenous scholar and a community member. At the beginning stages of my PhD journey, I listened to my intuition (spirit guide) for direction. In Michel's (2012, 128) compelling description of storywork, she states: "*Indigenous Storywork* ... helped deepen my understanding of how Indigenous values, such as relationship, can interconnect, and sometimes depart, from academic narrative research. Archibald empowers the powerful processes of learning that traditional stories evoke."

I found that Indigenous storywork supported my understanding of how traditional stories and practices contributed to my deeper understanding of who I am. I understand why my autobiographical narrative is an important element of Secwépemc identity transmission, because "our research interests come out of our own narrative of experience and shape our narrative inquiry plotlines" (Clandinin and Connelly 2000, 121). By including myself in the plotline, I also needed to respect the traditions; Archibald helped me with this. With Archibald's guidance and support, I was able to sort through and express my lived experiences. Indigenous storywork facilitated the important traditional teachings that extended from our collective stories while honouring our traditional teachers – our Elders and grandparents.

The self-actualization of three generations of Secwépemc identities is a process of acknowledging the importance of our ways of knowing and ways of being. The shift from a Eurocentric to a Secwépemc worldview aligns with Wilson's (2008) Indigenous Knowledge lens, converting to an Indigenous paradigm rather than an Indigenous perspective. For me, the shift from perspective to paradigm means that as a Secwépemc person, I can articulate and express our collective stories from an embodied Secwépemc position (ontology) as opposed to a distant, abstract perspective. Learning from the actual experiences and lives of Secwépemc people is vital. The Secwépemc Hand Drum accentuates cultural protocols and the integrity and respect that is needed to maintain the linkages to our culture. It is strictly necessary that others understand the relationality between cultural norms and identity. To further support protocols, three of Archibald's seven principles set out in Indigenous storywork are significant, namely, "holism, interrelatedness, and synergy" (2008, 2); it was these that guided the story sharing. Archibald (2008, 11) explains holism as "an Indigenous philosophical concept of holism refer[ring] to the interrelatedness between the intellectual, spiritual (metaphorical values and beliefs and the Creator), emotional and physical." I honoured my holistic sphere (depicted in Figure 1.3), which includes self, family, community, Elders, and the Creator, and I embraced heart, mind, body, and spirit. The circular Hand Drum wholeheartedly represents holism. The interrelatedness and synergy brings identity, home, and community together.

Reverberations from the Hand Drum

For the Secwépemc people, the Hand Drum is very important and sacred. The drum connects us to community and reminds us of our cultural values. I learned how to lead a song, and with support and practice, I became stronger. I am honouring the Hand Drum and our cultural ways by learning songs from our nation. This is my way of giving back.

There were times when the writing process got painful and I got stuck. When this happened, I reached for my Hand Drum to comfort me. I listen to the reverberations of the drumstick as it strokes the surface of the drum and the motions and sounds help me to realize the intentions of my work. I respect the integrity of the Hand Drum, which brings me back to my humble beginnings and it helps me move from my head to my heart. I will continue to learn how to sing Secwépemc songs and speak the Secwepemctsín language.

Benefits of Knowing One's Identity

Elder Jean, Colten, and I benefited from the opportunity to express what Secwépemc identity means to us, and it gave us the opportunity to express our truth. Jean's narrative shows strength and commitment in the practice and passing on of traditions; Colten shares valuable experiences regarding the perceptions of youth in schools, in communities, and with family; and I now have a greater appreciation for how my relationship with my grandparents sustained my cultural identities.

The insights gained are invaluable for understanding the strength and resilience of the Secwépemc people. The stories contained in this book dispel the myths exposed by Furniss (1999) that Secwépemc people were invisible around Williams Lake. Ignace (2008) took a stand, claiming that Secwépemc people have a foundation and history that authenticates our existence. As more Secwépemc storytellers come forward, we can collectively reverse the description of our history as crafted by non-Indigenous academics. Sharing our lives and stories is a beginning for many of us to heal and self-authenticate our cultural experiences.

I realize that I do have a strong sense of who I am (my identity) and who I am becoming, I just needed the courage, confidence, and space to express it. Through the reliving and retelling of my story, I identified how my grandparents passed on the strength of my Secwépemc identity through their teachings. I connected with the reality of separation from my mother by understanding that it was not her fault that I did not have a close relationship with her. The reflexivity helped me see my lived experiences in a healing way. I can turn the dark experiences that limited me into learning and teaching experiences that move me forward. For the first time, on Monday, October 14, 2013, I wept when I listened to the song "You Are My Sunshine," the same song my grandmother sang to me when I was a little girl. The words in the song connected me to how my grandparents must have felt about their daughter, and they were passing on the same love and affection to me. I am beginning to remove the self-destructive walls I had raised: I think there is someone with a lot more strength and compassion inside those walls. I am hoping that I had – and have – the ability to pass on important teachings to my children, just as my grandparents passed them on to me.

Positive, proactive, and sincere interest in understanding the past, present, and future of Secwépemc identities can assist teachers, caregivers, and service providers understand how to work and interact with Indigenous Peoples and others who have been confined by varying degrees of subjugation. I felt confined, and it took a lot of work and effort to advance to a place where I felt that my story mattered. By sharing our stories, we may help others get out from under the weight of their subjugation more quickly.

I Believe in Myself

When I began this journey, it was difficult to step outside of my comfort zone. Yet, I needed to place myself within the story to understand and relate to my past and connect to my people. Like Maenette Benham (2007), I related to how stories have the power to explore peoples' relationships publicly and privately, within their environment, and with one another. The stories illuminate knowledge that connects people to their roots as individuals and communally. My storied life with my grandparents taught me about the strong familial ties in my community, and I found that my grandparents loved me like they loved their daughter. I learned from Jean's story sharing that my mom was a wonderful person. If I had not gone through the storying process, I would not have come to make meaning of my past experiences, which help me to heal and believe in myself. I am sure many people will be able to relate to my story. It is through our Elders' teachings that Indigenous Peoples survived and were able to keep cultural knowledges intact.

Don't Ask Me to Bleed

I established how Secwépemc identities were, and are still, threatened to varying degrees by misguided history, legislation, colonialism, and the lost sense of who we are – individually and collectively. A huge chunk of our past has been taken from us, so telling and sharing these stories can be emotionally, physically, psychologically, and spiritually draining. To get there required a lot of courage and emotional strength.

In essence, it would be helpful for non-Indigenous people who live in Canada to learn and understand the impacts of our colonial history and the ensuing struggles we faced. The ideas presented in this book provides valuable awareness of how colonial atrocities have gravely affected us. In my lifetime, I have been exposed to Indian hospitals and residential school. These combined experiences could have destroyed me, but it was the teachings, strength, and support of my grandparents and Elders and my resilience that sustained me throughout life. For this, I am thankful to my grandparents, my ancestors, and the Creator; Kukstemc Tqelt Kukwipi7. My scars are emotional, psychological, and spiritual; they are internal rather than external. My story is not sensational, it does not bleed, so my story remained hidden, untold, and not newsworthy.

Sharing our Secwépemc stories is a giveaway for teaching. The sharing helps us to move away from the debilitating oppression of colonialism; as we continue to tell our stories, the knowledge grows. We saw this with the uncovering of the unmarked graves in Tk'emlúps te Secwépemc territory. I believe the children kicked the door open, and these accounts will be fully exposed. The truth telling will support the healing of our nations with reparations to the souls of those who are gone, the living, and those yet to come. In a sense, the curtain fell on Canada.

Notes

CHAPTER 1 • Drumming as Metaphor

1. I capitalize these terms in recognition of the high degree of honour the Hand Drum and Elders hold in Secwépemc culture.
2. Throughout my book, I privilege Secwépemc as my preferred identity marker. I also use "Secwépemc" interchangeably with "Indigenous" because I wish to proclaim and disrupt labels. The term "Indigenous" expresses my affinity with people globally who have similar backgrounds. This use of the term is supported by the United Nations. I use labels such as "Aboriginal," "Indian," "Native," and "First Nations" when citing authors or referring to legislative policy.
3. Shuswap is the English word for Secwépemc.
4. BC in particular has the most culturally and linguistically diverse Indigenous population and, therefore, knowing and understanding each nation and territory is important for establishing education and policy relationships.
5. In my study, the Hand Drum serves dual purposes. It represents a strong sense of embodiment for me as I began to understand my Hand Drum as Secwépemc culture. The circular and physical features of the Hand Drum and its representation of spiritual connectedness to the land and ancestors guide me and remind me to stay strong in who I am.

CHAPTER 2 • The Drum Reverberates against the Intergenerational Aspects of Colonialism

1. The intertwining relationships will be discussed in more detail in the next chapter, where I expand on the metaphor of my first Hand Drum.

CHAPTER 4 • Elder Jean's Stories

1. Jean's interviews took place on August 10, 2011, September 11, 2011, and December 6, 2011. In this chapter, the interview dates are not cited in the text to maintain the narrative flow of the stories.

2   All names have been changed to ensure confidentiality.
3   Jean and Colten use Shuswap to define our genealogy, where I prefer Secwépemc.

CHAPTER 5 • Colten's Stories

1   Colten's interviews took place on August 10, 2011, September 11, 2011, and December 6, 2011. In this chapter, the interview dates are not cited in the text to maintain the narrative flow of the stories.

CHAPTER 6 • Intergenerational Knowledge Transmission

1   I included Elders with grandparents because grandparents can fulfill the role of an Elder but not all grandparents wish to be acknowledged as an Elder. To respect them, I do not automatically reference grandparents as Elders.
2   Due to the limitations and time constraints of my study, I did not delve into geography or place names within the territory. There are some names mentioned as Jean or Colten spoke about them during our conversations. A thorough account of Secwépemc history is captured in Ron Ignace's work, "Our Oral Histories Are Our Iron Posts: Secwépemc, Stories and Historical Consciousness" (2008). I utilize Ignace's dissertation for historical reference.
3   Other aspects of Secwépemc Knowledge that Ignace (2008) discusses are language, common history, and common laws. These latter areas were guided by the Secwépemc Elders, uniting the people through the common bonds of kinship and family relations within, and between, communities.

References

Absolon, Kathleen. 2011. *Kaandossiwin: How We Come to Know.* Winnipeg, MB: Fernwood Publishing.
Abu-Saad, Ismael. 2006. "State-Controlled Education and Identity Formation among the Palestinian Arab Minority in Israel." *American Behavioral Scientist* 49 (8): 1085–100.
Aluli-Meyer, Manulani. 2001. "Acultural Assumptions of Empiricism: A Native Hawaiian Critique." *Canadian Journal of Native Education* 25 (2): 188–98.
–. 2008. "Indigenous and Authentic: Hawaiian Epistemology and the Triangulation of Meaning." In *Handbook of Critical and Indigenous Methodologies*, edited by Norman K. Denzin, Yvonna S. Lincoln, and Linda Tuhiwai Smith, 217–32. London: SAGE.
Anderson, Beatrice Marie. 2011. "*Nlakapmux* Grandmothers' Traditional Teachings and Learnings." PhD diss., University of British Columbia.
Anderson, Kim. 2000. *A Recognition of Being: Reconstructing Native Womanhood.* Toronto: Sumach Press.
Archibald, Jo-ann. 1997. "Coyote Learns to Make a Storybasket: The Place of First Nations Stories in Education." PhD diss., Simon Fraser University.
–. 2008. *Indigenous Storywork: Educating the Heart, Mind, Body, and Spirit.* Vancouver: University of British Columbia Press.
Atleo, Eugene Richard. 2004. *Tsawalk: A Nuu-chah-nulth Worldview.* Vancouver: University of British Columbia Press.
Battiste, Marie. 2000. *Reclaiming Indigenous Voice and Vision.* Vancouver: University of British Columbia Press.
Benham, Maenette. 2007. "*Mo'ōlelo*: On Culturally Relevant Story Making from an Indigenous Perspective." In *Handbook of Narrative Inquiry: Mapping a Methodology*, edited by D. Jean Clandinin, 512–34. Thousand Oaks, CA: SAGE.
Billy, Janice R. 2009. "Back from the Brink: Decolonizing through the Restoration of Secwépemc Language, Culture, and Identity." PhD diss., Simon Fraser University.
Blaeser, Kimberly M. 1999. "Writing Voices Speaking: Native Authors and an Oral Aesthetic." In *Talking on the Page: Editing Aboriginal Oral Texts*, edited by Laura J. Murray and Keren Rice, 53–68. Toronto: University of Toronto Press.

Brown, Francis Lee. 2004. "Making the Classroom a Healthy Place: The Development of Affective Competency in Aboriginal Pedagogy." PhD diss., University of British Columbia.

Bruno, Shauna Lynn. 2010. "Nehiyawiskwew Âcimowina: Attending to the Silences in the Lives of Cree Women in University." PhD diss., University of Alberta.

Cajete, Gregory. 1994. *Look to the Mountain: An Ecology of Indigenous Education.* Santa Fe, NM: Clear Light.

–. 2000. "Indigenous Knowledge: The Pueblo Metaphor of Indigenous Education." In *Reclaiming Indigenous Voice and Vision*, edited by Marie Battiste, 181–91. Vancouver: University of British Columbia Press.

Cardinal, Trudy. 2010. "For All My Relations: An Autobiographical Narrative Inquiry into the Lived Experiences of One Aboriginal Graduate Student." Master's thesis, University of Alberta.

Clandinin, D. Jean, and Michael F. Connelly. 2000. *Narrative Inquiry: Experience and Story in Qualitative Research.* San Francisco: Jossey-Bass.

Dewey, John. 1938. *Experience and Education: The Kappa Delta Pi Lecture Series.* New York: Collier Books.

Duran, Eduardo. 2006. *Healing the Soul Wound: Counseling with American Indians and Other Native Peoples.* New York: Teachers College Press.

Favrholdt, Kenneth. 2001. "The Mythological History of the Shuswap." *The Secwépemc News*, December.

Frideres, James. 2008. "Aboriginal Identity in the Canadian Context." *The Canadian Journal of Native Studies* 28 (2): 313–42.

Furniss, Elizabeth. 1995. *Victims of Benevolence: The Dark Legacy of the Williams Lake Residential School.* Vancouver: Arsenal Pulp Press.

–. 1999. *The Burden of History: Colonialism and the Frontier Myth in a Rural Canadian Community.* Vancouver: University of British Columbia Press.

Goudreau, Ghislaine, Cora Weber-Pillwax, Sheila Cote-Meek, Helen Madill, and Stan Wilson. 2008. "Hand Drumming: Health-Promoting Experiences of Aboriginal Women from a Northern Ontario Urban Community." *International Journal of Indigenous Health* 4 (1): 72–83.

Grande, Sandy. 2008. "Red Pedagogy: The Un-Methodology." In *Handbook of Critical and Indigenous Methodologies*, edited by Norman K. Denzin, Yvonna S. Lincoln, and Linda Tuhiwai Smith, 223–54. London: SAGE.

Holmes, Leilani. 2000. "Heart Knowledge, Blood Memory, and the Voice of the Land: Implications of Research among Hawaiian Elders." In *Indigenous Knowledges in Global Contexts: Multiple Readings of Our World*, edited by George J. Sefa Dei, Budd L. Hall, and Dorothy Goldin Rosenberg, 37–53. Toronto: University of Toronto Press.

Ignace, Ron. 2008. "Our Oral Histories are Our Iron Posts: Secwépemc, Stories and Historical Consciousness." PhD diss., Simon Fraser University.

Kirkness, Verna J., and Ray Barnhardt. 1991. "First Nations and Higher Education: The Four R's – Respect, Relevance, Reciprocity, Responsibility." *The Journal of American Indian Education* 30 (3): 1–15.

Kuokkanen, Rauna. 2007. *Reshaping the University: Responsibility, Indigenous Epistemes, and the Logic of the Gift.* Vancouver: University of British Columbia Press.

Lessard, Sean Michael. 2010. "'Two-Stones' Stories: Shared Teachings through the Narrative Experiences of Early School Leavers." Master's thesis, University of Alberta.

Martin, Georgina. 2007. "The Erosion of the Rights of Indigenous People to Self-Determine Their Identity." Master's thesis, University of Northern British Columbia.

McIvor, Madeleine Karen. 2010. "Aboriginal Post-Secondary Education Policy Development in British Columbia, 1986–2011." PhD diss., University of British Columbia.

McIvor, Onowa. 2012. "*ikakwiy nihiyawiyân*: I Am Learning [to be] Cree." PhD diss., University of British Columbia.

Meijer Drees, Laurie. 2013. *Healing Histories: Stories from Canada's Indian Hospitals*. Edmonton: University of Alberta Press.

Michel, Kathryn A. 2012. "Trickster's Path to Language Transformation: Stories of *Secwépemc* Immersion from Chief Atahm School." PhD diss., University of British Columbia.

Monchalin, Lisa. 2016. *The Colonial Problem: An Indigenous Perspective on Crime and Injustice in Canada*. Toronto: University of Toronto Press.

Nakata, Martin. 2007. *Disciplining the Savages: Savaging the Disciplines*. Canberra, AU: Aboriginal Studies Press.

Narine, Shari. 2023. "Author Wab Kinew Reaches Out to His Young Audience through Their Virtual Worlds." Windspeaker, https://windspeaker.com/news/windspeaker-news/author-wab-kinew-reaches-out-his-young-audience-through-their-virtual-world. Accessed June 4, 2024.

Palmer, Andie Diane N. 1994. "Maps of Experience: Shuswap Narratives of Place." PhD diss., University of Washington.

richardson, rupert. 2012. "writing as ceremony." EDST 585, University of British Columbia, student capstone paper, April.

Rosborough, Patricia Christine. 2012. "Ḵangex̱tola Sewn-on-Top: Kwak'wala Revitalization and Being Indigenous." PhD diss., University of British Columbia.

Sandy, Nancy Harriet. 2011. "Reviving Secwépemc Child Welfare Jurisdiction." Master's thesis, University of Victoria.

Schneider, Joyce. 2007. "Whispering the Circle Back: Participating in the Oral Transmission of Knowledge." Master's thesis, University of Northern British Columbia.

–. 2008. "4th Presentation: Joyce Schneider's Story, 'Whispering the Circle Back' (with Suzanne Stewart and Carole LeClair)." In *The Authentic Dissertation: Alternative Ways of Knowing, Research, and Representation*, edited by Donald Trent Jacobs, 33–39. London: Routledge.

Sellars, Bev. 2013. *They Called Me Number One: Secrets and Survival at an Indian Residential School*. Vancouver: Talonbooks.

Smith, Graham Hingangaroa. 1997. "The Development of Kaupapa Maori: Theory and Praxis." PhD diss., University of Auckland.

Smith, Linda Tuhiwai. 1999. *Decolonizing Methodologies: Research and Indigenous Peoples*. NY: Zed Books.

–. 2005. "On Tricky Ground: Researching the Native in the Age of Uncertainty." In *The Sage Handbook of Qualitative Research*, 3rd ed., edited by Norman K. Denzin and Yvonna S. Lincoln, 85–107. Thousand Oaks, CA: SAGE.

–. 2010. "Keynote Address." Presentation, Indigenous Studies 10th Anniversary, Celebrating Indigenous Knowledges: Peoples, Lands, Cultures. Trent University, Peterborough, ON, June 16–20.

Steinhauer, Patricia. 2001. "Situating Myself in Research." *Canadian Journal of Native Education*, 25 (2): 183–87.

Vanier, Jean. 1998. *Becoming Human*. Toronto: House of Anansi Press.

Wilson, Shawn. 2008. *Research Is Ceremony: Indigenous Research Methods*. Halifax, NS: Fernwood Publishing.

Young, Mary Isabelle. 2003. "Pimatisiwin: Walking in a Good Way – A Narrative Inquiry into Language as Identity." PhD diss., University of Alberta.

Index

Note: "(i)" after a page number indicates an illustration. In subentries, Elder Jean William is referred to as "Elder Jean," and Colten Wycotte as "Colten."

100 Mile House, 67, 70
150 Mile House, 66, 106
150 Mile House Hotel, 86–87

"Aboriginal" (term): in Constitution Act, 26; vs inclusivity/global use of "Indigenous," 8, 133*n*2
Absolon, Kathleen, 24, 25, 34–35
Abu-Saad, Ismael, 124–25
affection, difficulties in showing, 10–11, 31, 49, 58; and author's early separation from mother, 10, 20, 30–31, 48–49, 52; as contrasted with Colten's love for grandmother/family members, 114–15, 119; and intergenerational trauma, 10–11, 77, 96; and nonphysical contact, 50, 57–58, 80. *See also* emotion(s); love
Alexis Creek, 103
Alkali Lake, 3
Aluli-Meyer, Manulani, 19, 27, 31
ancestors, guidance of, 31, 131; Hand Drumming and, 20, 28, 41, 48
Anderson, Beatrice Marie, 42
Anderson, Kim, 31, 41
animals: as thanked/respected for their sacrifice, 28, 32, 43. *See also* cattle; deer hunting; hides, deer or moose; horses; moose hunting
Archibald, Jo-ann (Q'um Q'um Xiiem), 7, 13, 23; foreword by, xi–xiv; on holism, 14, 16, 41, 129; Indigenous Knowledges and Education course taught by, 16–17, 28; *Indigenous Storywork: Educating the Heart, Mind, Body, and Spirit*, 22, 25, 29–30, 45, 74, 99, 128–29; on Stó:lō basket makers, 122; and story of Coyote searching for the bone needle, 43–44. *See also* Sto:lō Nation
Asahal Lake, 93
Atleo, Eugene Richard, 23–24; on interconnectedness of mind, body, and spirit, 15–16, 19, 41. *See also* holism, *and entry following*; relational sphere, of Indigenous holism

Barnhardt, Ray. *See* Kirkness, Verna J.
basket making, 89, 90(i), 91; and tradition of giving away first basket, 122
baskets: for berry picking, 84, 91; culinary arts, as filled with food gifts, 87; as given to Elder Jean's bereaved grandmother, 78, 87; as given to Elder Jean's grandfather,

76–77; Secwépemc, 89, 90(i), 91; as woven by author, 34
Battiste, Marie, 24
belonging, author's lost sense of, xv, 3, 4, 30; and early school experiences, 65, 72; as eased by childhood tricycle gift, 59, 72; as restored by Hand Drum/daughter's poem, 25, 71–73; as sustained by sharing of stories/familial connectedness, 73, 121, 123–24
Benham, Maenette, 131
bereavement: care of persons suffering, 87, 88; practices during, 78–79. *See also* funerals; mourning customs
berry picking, 37, 75, 93, 104, 105; baskets for, 84, 91; pausing of, as mourning custom, 78, 87. *See also* seasonal food gathering
Billy, Janice R., 125
Blaeser, Kimberly M., 30
bloodline: kinship as extending beyond, 78, 86
blood memory, 41, 71; in Hawaiian culture, 35. *See also* memories
Brown, Francis Lee, 49
Bruno, Shauna Lynn, 18
Building Peaceful Communities Summer Institute (University of Alberta), 19–20, 50
bush (traditional) food, 91, 92. *See also* berry picking; deer hunting; moose hunting; seasonal food gathering; subsistence practices

Cajete, Gregory, 8, 16, 19, 22, 24
Campbell River, 101, 103
Canoe Creek (reserve community), 96
Cardinal, Bob, 20, 45
Cardinal, Trudy, 46
care: of bereaved persons, 78, 87, 88; of Elders, by community, 82–83; of grandchildren, by grandparents, 6, 13, 26–27, 50–66, 71, 79–80, 81, 127; of grandparents, by grandchildren, 68–69, 81, 82, 83; in hospitals outside community, 57, 60, 83; of stories, 45–46, 47
Cariboo College (now Thompson Rivers University, Kamloops), 69–70

Cariboo Indian Student Residence (formerly St. Joseph's Mission), 66–69; author as boarder at, 4, 10, 66–68, 92, 131; crest of, 68, 68(i)
Carrier (Dakelh) (people), 76, 78; basket made by, as given to Elder Jean's grandfather, 76–77; as residential school students, 66
Catholic Church: and behaviour/subjects considered taboo, 58; Christmas events introduced by, 60, 95; and dowry, as introduced by nuns, 76; and faith of Elder Jean's grandparents, 85; and faith/spirituality of author's grandmother, 58, 86. *See also* residential school(s); St. Joseph's Mission
cattle, 79, 91, 93
ceremonies, 31–32; Hand Drumming and, 32, 40–41
— Colten on: coming-of-age, 104, 105; Yuwipi (full moon), 105, 106
chief(s): Colten's father as, 109, 110; Elder Jean's dissatisfaction with, 97; Elder Jean's grandfather as consulted by, 83–84. *See also* leadership
Chilcotin (people): culture of, in Nemaiah, 104, 106, 119, 126; language of, as spoken by Colten, 106–7, 119; as residential school students, 66; stories of, as heard by Colten, 106
childbirth: author's separation from her mother at, xiii, xv, 4–6, 10, 18, 20, 27, 30–31, 49, 52, 53; housing of expectant mothers in preparation for, by author's grandparents, 60
children: as cared for/raised by grandparents, 6, 13, 26–27, 50–66, 71, 79–80, 81, 127; of large families/from different marriages, 77–78, 101–3; safety of, on reserves, 63, 66, 85, 101, 102, 123; showing affection to, 50, 52, 58, 80; unmarked graves of, as discovered at residential schools, 132. *See also entry below*; intergenerational knowledge transmission; intergenerational trauma; residential school(s)
chores, childhood: at home, 36–37, 63, 81, 84–85, 97–98; and joy of receiving appreciation, 97; at residential school, 67. *See also* work ethic

Christmas, 58, 59, 102; gift-giving at, 60, 95–96; sleigh ride/midnight dinner at, 122–23

Clandinin, D. Jean, and Michael F. Connelly, 7, 22, 50, 128

collective, Secwépemc society as. *See* community

collective storywork/life histories, xi, 6–8, 14–15, 30, 39, 119–20, 121–28. *See also* Martin, Georgina, stories told by; William, Elder Jean, stories told by; Wycotte, Colten, stories told by

colonialism: of academia, 16–18, 38, 70–71; and Indigenous Peoples of the world, 8, 124–25, 133*n*2; and loss of cultural identity, xv, 6–7, 9–11, 15, 22–23, 41–42, 124–28, 131. *See also* Indian Act (1876); Indian day schools (on-reserve); Indian hospitals; intergenerational trauma; reserves; residential school(s)

Columneetza Senior High School (Williams Lake): author as student at, 11, 54, 58, 68, 111, 112, 117, 118

coming-of-age ceremony: Colten on, 104, 105

community: care of Elders in, 82–83; ceremonies/collective experiences in, 105–6; cohesion/support in, 75–76, 88, 92–94, 95, 122–23; Elders' role in, 83–84, 123–24, 125; food supply of, 91–94; health care in hospitals outside, 57, 60, 83; in holistic ontology, 19; and identity, 8–9, 10, 41–43; and Indigenous Knowledge, 21–22; and Indigenous research/protocols, 23–24, 28, 42, 46; leaders of, 33, 83–84, 97, 109, 110; position of, in relational sphere, 11, 15, 15(i), 41, 129; self-sufficiency of, 75–76, 92; work ethic of, 84–85, 98; youth mentorship/support in, 109, 110, 111

Constitution Act (1982): use of "Aboriginal" in, 26

convent, of St. Joseph's Mission, 67; author's father as raised at, 10, 77

Coqualeetza (Qw'oqw'elith'a): reclamation of community at, xiii–xiv. *See also* entry below

Coqualeetza Indian Hospital (Sardis): author's birth/separation from her mother at, xiii, xv, 4–6, 10, 18, 20, 27, 30–31, 49;

author's mother quarantined for tuberculosis at, xv, 5–6, 30, 52, 53, 63, 77; author's removal from, into grandparents' care, 6, 127; closure of, xiii; as former residential school, 30; lands of, as reclaimed by Sto:lō Elders, xiii–xiv; Sellars's admission to, 127

courage, 21, 30, 102; to perform on Hand Drum, 17; to share stories, xii, 130, 131; to show affection, 58

cousins: of Colten, 103, 105, 114, 118; of Elder Jean, 77, 86

"Coyote Searching for the Bone Needle" (trickster story), 43–45

cranes, 106

Creation: Indigenous Knowledge/worldviews and, 24, 34–35; place names, in stories of, 122

Creator, 31; honouring of, 39; offering/prayer to, as preceding hunt/food gathering, 32; position of, in relational sphere, 11, 15, 15(i), 41, 129; prayers of thanks to, x, 85, 86, 96, 131

cultural identity/identities, xi, xii, xiii, 6–11, 17–19, 122–28; as defined by stories, 7–8, 19, 73, 98–99, 122–24, 126–27, 128, 130; and homeland, 27, 126, 128; and Indigenous Knowledge, xv, 10, 21–22, 24–25, 27, 28, 35, 45, 128–29; loss of, xv, 6–7, 9–11, 15, 22–23, 41–42, 124–28, 131; need to reclaim ownership of, 18–19, 27–28; and Secwépemc pedagogy, 15, 24–25; and Secwépemc survival, 42–43, 98–99, 124, 128; as shaped by Elders/grandparents, 7, 10, 98–99, 121, 123–26, 130

cultural protocols: of academic research with/for Indigenous Peoples, xv, 14, 23–24; of Hand Drum, xv–xvi, 24, 31, 40, 129; of sharing circles, 19, 40

cultural values, 9, 23–24; Hand Drum and, 16, 129

dances, 31, 32, 88, 93, 105

day schools, Indian (on-reserve), 4, 27, 126; author as student at, 55, 55(i), 64, 66

deer hunting, 22, 91; and *Alphonse* case, 9; Colten's photo/experiences of, 100, 101, 106, 117, 123; and hunter's thanks/

respect for animal's sacrifice, 28, 43; and sharing of meat, 93, 94; timing of, for making Hand Drum, 28, 46. *See also* hides, deer or moose

detachment, issues of, 5, 52, 119

Dewey, John, 36

discipline, 79, 84–85. *See also* chores, childhood; work ethic

disruption(s), of Indigenous culture/identity, 5, 9–11, 47, 124, 127

dowry (wedding): as practice introduced by nuns, 76

dreams: in coming-of-age ceremony, 104, 105; visions seen in, 105–6

Drees, Laurie Meijer: *Healing Histories: Stories from Canada's Indian Hospitals*, 5–6, 127

driving: in care/support of family members/friends, 69, 118, 123

drum, Indigenous. *See* Hand Drum; little boy water drum

Duran, Eduardo, 18, 77

education. *See* Indian day schools (on-reserve); Martin, Georgina, early education of, *and* postsecondary education of; residential school(s); schools, Colten's experiences of; *entries for specific schools and universities*

Elders: care of, in community, 82–83; as preserving/passing on Secwépemc knowledge, 124–25, 134n3; as shaping cultural identity, 7, 10, 98–99, 121, 123–26, 130; as teaching traditional cultural practices, 104–5, 114. *See also* grandfathers; grandmothers; grandparents; Moiese, Ned and Nancy; William, Elder Jean

elk hide, 28; author's rattle made from, 34

emotion(s), as experienced by author, xv, 4, 14, 29, 59, 131–32; and connection to grandparents, 36, 50–51, 53, 57–58, 79–80; and difficulties in showing affection, 10–11, 20, 31, 49, 50, 58, 77; and early separation from mother, 5, 10, 18, 20, 30–31, 48–49, 52; and intergenerational trauma, 10–11, 18, 77, 119; and sound of Hand Drum, 41

Esket (Esk'etemc), 93; Wycotte family and, 94–95

familial relationships, 123–24, 126, 131; Colten on, 101–4, 115, 118, 119, 122, 126; Elder Jean on, 77–79, 86; non-physical contact and, 50, 57–58, 80

family, xii, 14, 26–27, 46, 52; position of, in relational sphere, 11, 15, 15(i), 41, 129. *See also* intergenerational knowledge transmission; kinship, of Secwépemc

— disruptions to, as caused by European contact/colonialism: of fur trade, 125; of Indian hospitals, xii, xiii, 4–6, 27, 126, 127; of residential schools, xii, xiii, 40, 41–42, 56. *See also* intergenerational trauma; residential school(s); separation

family cohesion: and community work ethic/support, 75–76, 84–85, 91–94; Elder Jean on, 75–76, 77–79, 81, 86, 122–23; and grandparents' raising of grandchildren, 81

fasting/dreaming ritual, for youth, 104, 105

First Nations House of Learning (UBC), 17

fishing, 42, 83, 84, 128; Colten's experiences of, 101, 104, 105, 112, 113, 114; with dip nets, 107, 113; fur trade's effects on, 125; monitoring of, 107–8, 113; as sustainable, 93, 94, 107; Wycotte family area for, 87–88. *See also* salmon; subsistence practices

food. *See* berry picking; fishing; hunting; seasonal food gathering; subsistence practices

— sharing of, 91–92; as gifts, 87, 95; with those in need, 75, 92–94

— traditional (bush), 91, 92; vs processed/store-bought, 92, 95

food chain, 93, 94

food supply, of households/community, 91–94

four Hs (Secwépemc attributes/values), 39–40; honour, 39, 48–49; hope, 39–40; humility, 13, 33, 39, 48–49; humour, 40, 48–49; as represented on Hand Drum, 35, 35(i)

four Rs (respect, relevance, reciprocity, responsibility), as representing Indigenous students' educational needs, 23

framework, for Indigenous research: as culturally embedded/relevant, 24, 37; Hand Drum and, 24, 32–35, 34(i), 35(i);

holistic embodiment and, 15(i), 15–16; Indigenous Knowledge and, 21
Fraser River: Elder Jean on fish camp at, 87–88
Frideres, James, 126
full moon (Yuwipi) ceremony: Colten on, 105, 106
funerals: of Colten's grandfather, 103; of Elder Jean's brother, 87; song sung at, 32. *See also* bereavement; mourning customs
fur trade, 125
Furniss, Elizabeth, 7, 9; *The Burden of History: Colonialism and the Frontier Myth in a Rural Canadian Community*, 127, 130

gardens: and fields, as promised to Elder Jean's grandfather, 76, 95; vegetable, 91, 92
genealogy, 41, 99
generations. *See* intergenerational knowledge transmission; intergenerational trauma
gifts: by author to Colten, in gratitude for story-sharing, 100; of author's childhood tricycle, 59–60, 72; of author's first Hand Drum, 3–4, 32–34, 34(i), 35(i); of author's second Hand Drum, 32, 33(i); baskets as, 76, 78, 87, 89, 122; and celebrations, as not part of Secwépemc practice, 95–96; at Christmas, 59, 60, 95, 96; at cultural gatherings, xii, xiv, 40; of food, xiv, 87, 95; grandparents/teachings as, 52, 60, 62–63, 71, 79–80
Glanfield, Florence, 19
good character, 33, 52
Grande, Sandy, 38
grandfathers
— of author, 6(i), 44–45, 51(i), 55–63, 64, 65, 66, 68–69, 71, 76; and advice to "never forget who you are/where you come from," 10, 13, 14, 38, 42, 45, 47, 68; and encouragement to get an education/bring it back to the people, 11, 42–43, 70; on hospitality/sharing, 38–39, 60; manual labour by, 36–37, 51, 54, 62; work ethic taught by, 13, 36–37, 63. *See also* grandparents; Moiese, Ned and Nancy
— of Colten, 103, 117, 118; hunting/fishing with, 100, 101, 106, 114, 123
— of Elder Jean, 76–79, 81–84, 91; care of, in later life, 82; as community advisor, 83–84; marriages of, 76, 78–79, 94–95; and work at St. Joseph's Mission, 77, 96; and work ethic of chores/traditional activities, 84, 88, 93, 97; and work with horses, 81
grandmothers, 32, 41
— of author, 6(i), 51(i), 55–63, 64, 66, 69; berry picking/cooking by, 36, 37, 62; Catholic faith of, 58–59, 86; hide preparation by, 29; singing by, 80, 130; and trips to sweathouse, 89. *See also* grandparents; Moiese, Ned and Nancy
— of Colten, 103, 117–18; "hanging out" with/learning traditional activities from, 114–15; on spiritual experiences/signs, 105, 106, 114
— of Elder Jean, 77–80, 82, 85–88, 92; faith/spirituality of, 85–86; illness/death of, 83; love shown by, 80; marriages of, 76, 78–79, 87, 94–95; siblings of, 77–78; and work ethic of chores/traditional activities, 84, 87, 88, 93, 97
grandparents: care of, by grandchildren, 68–69, 81, 82, 83; care of grandchildren by, 6, 13, 26–27, 50–66, 71, 79–80, 81, 127; cultural identity as shaped by, 7, 10, 98–99, 121, 123–26, 130; faith/spirituality of, 58, 85, 86; as gifts, 52, 60, 62–63, 71, 79–80; Hand Drum's connectedness with, 13, 19, 20, 31, 41; Hand Drum's handle, as representing, 35, 35(i), 36–40, 124; and Indigenous knowledge, 20, 35, 38, 122; love of, 81, 130; respect for, 59, 69, 82–84, 97–98, 111, 114; respect as taught/practised by, 27, 45, 52, 79–80; strong relationships with, 81–82, 123–24; Traditional Knowledge/teachings of, 39, 87–89, 121–22, 126; values taught by, 13, 36, 52, 71, 79–80. *See also* Elders; Moiese, Ned and Nancy; teachings, by Elders/grandparents; William, Elder Jean

Hampton, Eber, 43
Hand Drum: author's first, as gifted to her by her friend, 3–4, 32–34, 34(i), 35(i); and author's identity, 4, 7, 33–35, 47, 129; and author's journey through academia, 4, 16–17, 20, 24, 28, 40, 44, 47, 128;

author's learning to play, 17, 20, 28, 34, 43, 47, 71, 126, 129; author's second, as gifted to her by T'exelc Nation, 32, 33(i); as author's spirit guide, 4, 16–19, 25, 31, 41; care involved in creation of, 4, 29, 31, 46; care of, 33, 34, 43; circular shape of, as evoking holism, 129, 133n5; and connectedness with grandparents/ancestors, 13, 19, 20, 31, 41; and connectedness with land, 3, 4, 32, 43, 133n5; deer or moose hide used to create, 28–29, 43, 46; denigration of, as "barbaric," 47; as embodying Indigenous Knowledge, xv–xvi, 20, 24, 25, 28, 32–33, 35, 37–38, 41, 128, 129; four Hs as represented on, 35, 35(i); honouring of, 40, 43; as living/breathing with spirit of animal, 28–29; as made by author, 34; as metaphor, 31–35, 35(i); spirit of, 40–43; and Women's Warrior song, xi, 16–17, 71, 126
— handle of, 34(i): as made of antler, 124; as representing grandparents, 35, 35(i), 36–40, 124; and spider web of sinew straps, as representing intertwining relationships, 34–35

Hawaii, Indigenous Peoples of, 19, 35. *See also* Aluli-Meyer, Manulani; Holmes, Leilani

haying: Elder Jean's stories of, 84, 93, 94

healing, 18, 26, 119, 132; from childhood separation, 52, 130; Hand Drum and, 41; humour and, 40; sharing circles for, 19–20, 40; spirituality and, 85; stories and, 38, 74, 105, 106

health: academic/emotional, of Indigenous students, 103; and care in hospitals outside community, 57, 60, 83; giving thanks for, 85; traditional foods and, 92. *See also* Indian hospitals; tuberculosis

heart: Hand Drum and, 16, 17, 41; Indigenous Knowledge and, 19–25
— moving from head to, 20, 38; Indigenous storywork and, 45–46; Hand Drum and, 129

heart, mind, body, and spirit, connection of: Hand Drum and, 47, 129; holism and, 14, 129; Indigenous storywork and, xii, 15, 16, 22, 45, 74. *See also* holism, *and entry following*; storywork, Indigenous

"heart knowledge," 35

heart work, 20, 128

heshook-ish tsawalk (Nuu-chah-nulth), 15–16. *See also* holism, *and entry following*; relational sphere, of Indigenous holism

hides, deer or moose: curing of, 29, 37, 75; scraping/softening of, 28, 29, 46, 88, 114; tanning of, 29, 92, 104, 105, 114, 128; and timing of hunt, 28, 46; as used to make Hand Drum, 28–29, 43, 46; work involved in preparation of, 88, 92

holism: Archibald on, 14, 16, 41, 129. *See also entry below*

holistic thinking/ontology, Indigenous, 14, 24, 99; Creator and, 11, 15(i), 41, 129; relational sphere diagram of, 15(i), 15–16, 129; vs Western worldviews/policies, 16, 17, 18, 19

Holmes, Leilani, 35

home (cultural identity/belonging), xii, xiv, 41, 129; and author's academic/spiritual journey, 8–9, 13, 19, 23, 24–25, 44

homeland, Indigenous connection to: and author's Hand Drums, 31, 32, 34–35, 38; and author's memories of grandparents/ teachings, 10, 26, 31, 38, 122, 124; and cultural identity, 27, 126, 128; missing links to, 19; as lost by youth, 42; and "return to the land," 22. *See also* land, Secwépemc connection to; Secwépemc territory

horses, 79, 86, 91, 93; and Christmas sleigh rides, 122–23; Colten's experiences with, 108; feeding/watering of, 81; and travel with wagons, 38, 75, 81–82, 84, 85, 122

hospitals: in Vancouver, 83; in Williams Lake, 57, 60. *See also* Indian hospitals; Coqualeetza Indian Hospital

hunting: *Alphonse* case and, 9; Colten's stories of, 100, 101, 105, 106, 112, 113, 114, 123; Elder Jean's stories of, 75, 83, 84, 91, 92, 93, 94; offering/prayer to Creator preceding, 32. *See also* deer hunting; moose hunting; subsistence practices

identity/identities. *See* cultural identity/ identities

Ignace, Ron, "Our Oral Histories are Our Iron Posts: Secwépemc, Stories and

Historical Consciousness" (dissertation): on colonization/loss of Secwépemc culture, 124–25, 126; on importance of Elders in preserving/passing on Secwépemc knowledge, 124–25, 134n3; on Secwépemc history, 130, 134n2; on Secwépemc reciprocity, 39

independence: of author's grandparents, 69; of Colten, as supported by driver's licence, 118; of Secwépemc people, 98

Indian Act (1876): community name changed by, 12–13; cultural practices banned by, 9, 32, 126; hospitals sanctioned by, 5–6, 27, 126; Indigenous identities fabricated/imposed by, 5, 14, 18–19, 26, 27, 47, 126; and residential school system, 27, 126

Indian Agents, 97

Indian day schools (on-reserve), 4, 27, 126; author as student at, 55, 55(i), 64, 66

Indian hospitals, xii, xiii, 4–6, 27, 126; Drees on, 127. *See also* Coqualeetza Indian Hospital; intergenerational trauma

"Indigenous" (term): as preferred to "Aboriginal," 8, 133n2

Indigenous Knowledge: academic study of, 13, 24, 37–38; Archibald's course on, 16–17, 28; author's awakening to/renewed understanding of, 21–25; and author's grandparents, 20, 35, 38, 122; and author's sense of belonging, 25; and being at one with oneself, 41; Elder Jean's example of, 21–22; as embodied by Hand Drum, xv–xvi, 20, 24, 25, 28, 32–33, 35, 37–38, 41, 128, 129; as fluid/not linear, 22; from the heart, 19–25; as passed on through stories, 37–38, 74, 122; and Secwépemc identity/culture, xv, 10, 21–22, 24–25, 27, 28, 35, 45, 128–29; and story of Coyote searching for the bone needle, 43–45. *See also* intergenerational knowledge transmission; Traditional Knowledge; ways of knowing

Indigenous Peoples: and shared global experiences of colonialism, 8, 124–25, 133n2; United Nations Declaration on the Rights of, xiii

interference. *See* legislated interference

intergenerational knowledge transmission, xv, 44, 98–99; to author's children, 21–22; in communal story sharing by author, Elder Jean, and Colten, 14, 15, 28, 39, 121–32; as disrupted by ban on Indigenous languages, 9; in face of Western/colonial threats, 124–28; and Hand Drumming, 128–29; and Secwépemc identity/culture, 122–24, 130–31. *See also* Indigenous Knowledge; Traditional Knowledge; ways of knowing

intergenerational learning/teaching. *See entry above*; learning; teachings, by Elders/grandparents

intergenerational trauma, xi, 10–11, 71; defence mechanisms used to deal with, 10–11, 31; disease/"dis-ease" of, 26, 28; Duran on, 18, 77; and healing power of humour, 40; of Indian day schools, 4, 27, 126; of Indian hospitals/author's birth experience, xiii, 4–6, 10, 18, 27, 49, 52; as internalized, 96, 131–32; of residential schools, xiii, 4–5, 8, 10, 18, 27, 96, 104, 119

intermarriage/migration, Wycotte family and, 94–95

internalized trauma, 96, 131–32

interrelatedness: as principle of Indigenous storywork, xii, 99, 129

jam making and gifting: Elder Jean's stories of, 87, 95

James, Florence, 40

Kinew, Wab, 100

kinship, of Secwépemc, 9, 126, 134n3; and family/community cohesion, 75–76, 77–79, 81, 122–23; as not based solely on blood, 78, 86

Kirkness, Verna J., 13; and Ray Barnhardt, 23

knowledge. *See* Indigenous Knowledge; intergenerational knowledge transmission; Traditional Knowledge; ways of knowing

Kuokkanen, Rauna, 15

Lake Babine Nation, 70; author as member of, 12

land, Secwépemc connection to, xii, xv, 3, 4, 19, 20, 21–22, 79, 84, 105, 125, 128; and education/pedagogy, 13, 17, 104; and

Hand Drum, 4, 31–32, 43; and language, 15; and living off the land, 15, 32, 56, 75, 91–94, 106; and "return to the land," 21–22, 122, 124. *See also* homeland, Indigenous connection to

landscape(s): of author's childhood/school days, 55(i), 55–66, 71–73; of Colten's high school experiences, 109–12; of Secwépemc identities, as changed by European contact/settlement, 125; sharing of stories/life histories, as helping to change, 31

language(s), Indigenous: as banned at day schools/residential schools, 4, 9, 27, 40, 42, 56, 126; Colten on, 106–7, 118, 119; Elder Jean on, 79, 88; identity and, 14–15, 42, 47; kinship and, 9; as spoken by author's schoolmates, 66. *See also* Secwepemctsín

leadership: of Elder Jean's grandfather, 83–84; and humility, 39; and mentorship of Colten's father, 109, 110; and selection of community leaders, 33. *See also* chief(s)

learning: emotions and, 49; as experiential/place-based, 17; from Indigenous Peoples, in future, 106. *See also* intergenerational knowledge transmission; teachings, by Elders/grandparents

legislated interference: author's birth and, xv, 5, 10; as historical/ongoing threat to Secwépemc identity/culture, 124–28

Lessard, Sean Michael, 19, 20; on care of stories, 46

little boy water drum, 41

lived experience(s): of author's grandparents, 60; of Elder Jean, 74, 82, 98–99; of Indigenous Peoples, xiv, 8, 10, 29–30, 38, 46, 122. *See also* William, Elder Jean; Wycotte, Colten

— telling of, by author, xv, 14, 16, 27, 29, 30, 46, 49–50, 98, 126; and autoethnography, 7; and defence mechanisms against trauma, 10–11; with good intentions, 4, 29; and Hand Drum, 4, 16, 35; and Indigenous Knowledge, 44; and Indigenous storywork, 128–29; and narrative inquiry, 46; positive outcomes of, 71, 72–73, 130. *See also* Martin, Georgina

Louie, Delores, 40

love: of basket makers, 89, 91; expressions of, 50, 52, 57–58, 80, 96, 114, 115, 119; and gift-giving, 95; of grandparents, 81, 130. *See also* affection, difficulties in showing; emotion(s)

making meaning: of author's life story, 43–45; of Hand Drum, 17, 31–35, 35(i); of oneself, using relational sphere, 15(i), 15–16; of stories, 43–45, 46–47; of stories told by Elder Jean and Colten, xi, 30, 31, 73, 74, 98–99, 100, 118–20, 124, 131. *See also* meaning

Manitowabi, Edna, 41

manual labour: by author's grandfather, 36–37, 51, 54, 62; reduced necessity for, with modern conveniences, 85, 97–98

Maori, 70. *See also* Smith, Linda Tuhiwai

Marie Sharp Elementary School (Williams Lake), 65

marriage(s), 12; and Colten's alternating between two families/cultures, 101–3, 122; early age of, for young women, 77; of Elder Jean's grandparents, 76, 78, 94–95; to persons outside community, 94–95

Martin, Georgina, 48–73; as announcing herself, 48–49; birth of, and separation from her mother, xiii, xv, 4–6, 10, 18, 20, 27, 30–31, 49, 52, 53; as cared for/raised by grandparents, 6, 13, 26–27, 50–66, 71, 127; childhood community of, 49; eldest daughter of, 22, 72; eldest son of, 22, 58; family of, 49; and later care/support of her grandparents, 68–69, 81, 83; as "little mischief" to grandparents, 56, 57; youngest daughter of, 52, 70; youngest son of, 60, 70. *See also* Hand Drum; Moiese, Ned and Nancy

— early education of: at day school, 55, 55(i), 64, 66; at elementary school, 65; at junior high school, 65, 66, 67–68; and recreation/"hanging out" with friends, 117; as residential school boarder, 4, 10, 18, 66–68, 92, 131; and school sports, 65, 68, 117; at senior high school, 11, 54, 58, 68, 111, 112, 117, 118; and streaming into nonacademic courses, 111; and trip to Europe, 67–68; and work at residential school, 68(i), 68–69

—postsecondary education of, 54, 69–73, 113; academic challenges of, 70–71; as single parent, 69–70, 72. *See also* Hand Drum

—postsecondary education of (specific): Bachelor of Arts (political science), 70; certificate, Administration of Aboriginal Governments, 70; diploma, Business Administration, 69–70; diploma, Public Sector Management, 70; Master of Arts (interdisciplinary studies), 70, 71; PhD (education), xi, 4, 10, 13, 42–43, 54, 71, 128

—stories told by, 36–37, 38–39, 55–63; of berry picking with grandmother, 37; of Christmas and Easter at church, 58, 60; of Christmas decorations/gift-giving, 59, 60, 95–96; of clothing worn as child, 58–59, 61; of doing chores/grandfather's reward, 36–37, 63; of fall on Red Hot Potbelly Stove, 56–57; of grandmother's Catholic faith, 58–59, 86; of grandparents' hospitality/generosity, 38–39, 60; of grandparents' one-room log house, 36, 56, 60, 62–63; of hanging on to grandfather's back pocket as they walked, 61–62, 71; of hugs/affection as taboo, 57, 58; of moose or deer hides being prepared, 37; of playing with wooden blocks, 61; of uncle's tricycle gift, 59–60, 61, 72

—and stories told by Elder Jean and Colten, xi, 6–8, 14–15, 30, 39, 119–20, 121–28. *See also* William, Elder Jean; Wycotte, Colten

matrilineal society, of Secwépemc, 94–95
McIvor, Madeleine Karen, 28
McIvor, Onowa, 8
meadow(s): haying at, 93; sweats at, 87; wild tea from, 75; winter activities at, 91
meaning: of Hand Drum, 17, 31–35, 35(i); of photo of author's grandparents, 50–54; of Secwépemc identity, 124–29. *See also* making meaning
memories: blood, 35, 41, 71; cell, 18, 47; of Colten, 100, 101; of Elder Jean, 76–77, 81–82, 84–85, 98–99; as evoked by Hand Drum, 41, 47

—author's: of mother, 87; narrative inquiry and, 46; of school days, 67–68, 72, 117

—of author's grandparents, 10, 13, 22, 29, 42, 71, 122, 124; as contained in Hand Drum handle, 35–38; as evoked by photo, 50–54; in retelling stories, 55–63
Michel, Kathryn A., 18, 125, 127, 128
moccasins, gloves, and jackets: as made from cured hides, 37, 75
Moiese, Ned and Nancy (author's maternal grandparents): author's photo of, 6, 6(i), 13, 20, 50–54, 51(i), 55–56; author's stories of, 29, 36–37, 38–39, 55–63, 68–69, 80, 86, 95–96; as caring for/raising author from birth to adolescence, 6, 13, 26–27, 50–66, 71, 127; as later cared for/supported by author, 68–69, 81, 83; one-room log house of, 36, 56, 60, 62–63; as represented by handle of author's Hand Drum, 35, 35(i), 36–40, 124. *See also* Martin, Georgina, stories told by
Monchalin, Lisa, 26
moose hunting, 22, 91, 93; and hunter's thanks/respect for animal's sacrifice, 28, 43; and sharing of meat, 93, 94; timing of, for making Hand Drum, 28, 46. *See also* hides, deer or moose
mourning customs, 78–79; dietary restrictions as, 78. *See also* bereavement; funerals
music. *See* Hand Drum; singing

Nakata, Martin, 25
Nanaimo Indian Hospital, 6
National Aboriginal Day, 10, 110
Nemaiah (reserve community), Colten's experiences in: of alternating visits to, with visits to Sugar Cane, 102, 103; with friends/peers, 115; of rodeo "suicide race," 108; of schooling in, 102; of shadowing his father, 109; of traditional cultural practices, as taught by Elders/grandmother, 104–5, 114; of Yuwipi (full moon) ceremony, 105, 106

oral teachings: as received through stories, 98
oral tradition: Elder Jean on, 97; of teaching stories/educational reciprocity, 29–30
Owl and Coyote, story of, 43–45
owls, 88, 106, 114

Palestinians, 124–25
Palmantier, Kristy, 32

Palmantier, Monty, 70–71
Palmer, Andie Diane N.: on *Regina v. Alphonse*, 9
Paul, Herman: as maker of author's first Hand Drum, 33
Paul, Lena (author's friend), 89; as gifting author her first Hand Drum, 3–4, 32–33
pedagogy, Indigenous/Secwépemc, 13; as culture-/land-based, xv, 104; identity and, 15, 24–25; as means of dismantling colonialism, 38; storywork and, 44–45
PellTsko'ten (red rock used for making pipes), 122
personal care/grooming: of author, by grandparents, 80; of Elder Jean, by grandmother, 80; of grandfather, by Elder Jean, 82
photographs: of author, as child, 55, 55(i), 65, 71; of author's grandparents, 6, 6(i), 13, 20, 50–54, 51(i), 55–56; of Colten, on hunting trip, 100–1, 117; of Elder Jean's grandparents, 81–82
Pierre, Martina, 16. *See also* Women's Warrior song
potlatch, as banned by Indian Act, 9
Pow Wows, 10; Colten on, 105, 106; Elder Jean on, 88
power: of coming-of-age ceremony, 104, 105; of communal story sharing, 122; of Elder Jean's stories, 74; of Hand Drum, 13, 40–41, 47; of Indigenous knowledge, 38; of storywork, xiii, 128
— healing: of "good stories," 105–6; of humour, 40
Pratt, Don, 53
prayer, x, 85, 86; ceremonial, 104, 105; as preceding hunt/food gathering, 32
Prince George: author's home in, 11–12, 17, 50, 70; author's university work in, 70–71
protocols. *See* cultural protocols

quarantine, of author's mother, xv, 5–6, 30, 52, 53, 63, 77. *See also* Coqualeetza Indian Hospital
Q'um Q'um Xiiem. *See* Archibald, Jo-ann

racism: author's experiences of, 65; Colten's experiences of, 109; and Secwépemc loss of agency/voice/identity, 127

reciprocity: in Indigenous education, 23; in Indigenous storywork, xii, 29–30, 45; in Secwépemc culture, 39
Regina v. Alphonse (BC case), 9
relational sphere, of Indigenous holism, 15(i), 15–16, 129; position of Creator in, 11, 15(i), 41, 129. *See also* holism, *and entry following*
relationships: Indigenous storywork and, 45–46, 131; with nature/environment, 16, 24; nonphysical contact and, 50, 57–58, 80; ontological, 19; with others/"all of Creation," as signified by Hand Drum's handle, 34–35, 35(i), 36; reciprocal, 23. *See also* familial relationships
reserves: Catholic Church on, 58; children's sense of safety on, 63, 66, 85, 101–2, 123; day schools on, 4, 27, 126; permission needed to leave, 97; placement of Secwépemc on, after breakup of Nation into smaller communities, 124. *See also* day schools, Indian (on-reserve); Nemaiah; Sugar Cane
residential school(s): author as boarder at, 4, 10, 18, 66–68, 92, 131; author's father as raised at/student at, 10, 18, 77, 96; author's later work at, 68(i), 68–69; and banning of Indigenous languages, 9, 27, 40, 56, 126; Coqualeetza Indian Hospital as, 30; and discovery of unmarked children's graves, 132; Elder Jean at, 86; and healing power of humour, 40; and intergenerational trauma, xiii, 4–5, 8, 10, 18, 27, 96, 104, 119; and loss of Indigenous identity/culture, 9, 40, 41–42, 47, 56, 126; and separation from families/communities, xii, xiii, 40, 41–42, 56; siblings/cousins at, 56, 86; stories of, 96, 127. *See also* Indian day schools; intergenerational trauma
resilience: of author, 5, 66, 70–71, 131; of Secwépemc/Indigenous people, 39–40, 47, 124, 130
respect: for animals' sacrifice, 28, 32, 43; at community activities, 92–94; for grandparents/Elders, 59, 69, 82–84, 97–98, 111, 114; Hand Drum and, 4, 16, 33, 129; honour and, 39; in Indigenous research, 14, 23, 28, 30, 45–46; Indigenous storywork and, 29, 128–29; as leadership quality, 33; of sharing circles, 20; as

taught/practised by grandparents/Elders, 27, 45, 52, 79–80
responsibility: of expressing love, 80; of grandparents, in raising child, 53–54, 71, 81; of Hand Drumming, 4, 28, 32, 33, 43, 67; in Indigenous education, 23; in Indigenous storywork, xii, 44, 45, 99; as legacy of colonialism, 26, 38; of learning about one's culture, 126
retelling stories, 5, 98–99, 127; of author's care for grandparents, 69; of author's lived experiences, 16, 50, 55–63, 71, 73, 128, 130. *See also* Martin, Georgina, stories told by; William, Elder Jean; Wycotte, Colten
Richardson, Rupert, 26, 28
Rigney, Lester, 37
rodeo: author's uncle riding in, 55; "suicide race" in, at Nemaiah, 108; at Williams Lake Stampede, 69
Rosborough, Patricia Christine, 14–15, 28
Rudy Johnson Bridge: Colten's work at, 113

safety net/safety practices, in Indigenous communities, 81, 85, 102; and gun safety, 84, 123
salmon: as dried, 87, 92–93, 94; fishing of, as monitored, 107–8, 113; pause in handling of, as mourning custom, 78, 87; as salted, 92; as smoked, for protection from insects during drying process, 93, 94; as substituted for beaver during fur trade, 125; as sustainably harvested, 93, 94, 107; at T'exelc, 12. *See also* fishing
Salmon Valley River, 17
Sandy, Nancy Harriet, 12
Schneider, Joyce, 11, 41–42
schools. *See* Indian day schools; residential schools
— author's experiences of. *See* Martin, Georgina, early education of
— Colten's experiences of: as affected by alternating between two families, 101–3; and cultural practices, as taught in Nemaiah, 104; and First Nations support workers, 110, 111; at high school, 109–12; and languages, 107; and need for course upgrades, 109, 111; and subject interests, 109, 110, 112

Seabird (reserve community), 108
seasonal food gathering, 22, 32, 75, 91–93, 94. *See also* berry picking
Secwépemc: as matrilineal society, 94–95; prayer of, x; and "return to the land," 21–22, 122, 124. *See also* land, Secwépemc connection to; Shuswap (Secwépemc)
Secwépemc territory, 13; map of, 12(i); red rock as marker of, 122; reserve land on, as only small fraction of, 124
Secwepemctsín (language), 12, 125, 134*n*3; author's ability to speak, 27, 47, 66, 107, 112, 126, 129; author's announcement in, 48–49; Catholic prayers in, 58, 86; Colten's difficulties with, 107, 119. *See also* language(s), Indigenous
Sellars, Bev: *They Called Me Number One: Secrets and Survival at an Indian Residential School*, 127
separation: of author from her mother, at birth, xiii, xv, 4–6, 10, 18, 20, 27, 30–31, 49, 52, 53; from cultural identities, 8, 15, 41–42, 54; of grandchildren from siblings, 79–80; of parents, 101–3, 119, 122; of residential school students, from family/community, xii, xiii, 40, 41–42, 56
shadowing: by author, of her grandfather, 61; by Colten, of his father on chief's work, 109, 110
sharing circles, 19–20, 40
Sheep Creek: Colten as fish catch monitor at, 113
Sheep Creek Bridge, 103, 107
Shuswap (Secwépemc), 9, 96, 106, 133*n*3; 134*n*3; language of, 107, 119. *See also* Secwépemc, *and entries following*
siblings: of Colten, 115; at residential school, 56; Secwépemc relationships between, 77–78
— of author: childhood separation from, 53, 80; Elder Jean's caring role toward, 81, 86
singing, xii, 10, 31–32; to accompany Hand Drum, 4, 16, 32, 129; by author's grandfather, 81; by author's grandmother, 80, 130; by author's mother, 86; of Catholic hymns/rosary, 58; of Christmas carols, 60; at community events, 32; of Women's Warrior song, xi, 16–17, 71, 126; at Yuwipi (full moon) ceremony, 105

skateboarding: as youth recreational activity, 112, 113, 115, 116, 117, 127
Skeetchestn (reserve community), 108
Smith, Dorothy E., 49
Smith, Graham Hingangaroa, 24
Smith, Linda Tuhiwai, 13, 21–22, 24
social safety net, 102. *See also* safety net/safety practices, in Indigenous communities
spiritual guidance, 41, 84
spirituality, 85–86; Indigenous, as described by Colten, 105–6. *See also* Catholic Church; prayer
sports: author's experiences in, 65, 68, 117; Colten on, 108–9
St. Joseph Oblate House, 54
St. Joseph's Mission, 56, 66; author's father as raised at/as student at, 10, 18, 77, 96; discovery of unmarked graves at, 132; Elder Jean's grandfather as worker at, 77, 96. *See also* Cariboo Indian Student Residence
Sto:lō Nation: Archibald as member of, xii, 7, 17; and Coqualeetza lands, xiii–xiv; and tradition of basket maker giving away first basket, 122. *See also* Archibald, Jo-ann
stories: of Coyote searching for the bone needle, 43–45; of Creation, 122; good vs bad, 105–6. *See also entry below*; lived experience(s); Martin, Georgina, stories told by; retelling stories; William, Elder Jean; Wycotte, Colten
storywork, Indigenous: Archibald on, 22, 25, 29–30, 45, 74, 99, 128–29; as connecting heart, mind, body, and spirit, xii, 15, 16, 22, 45, 74; interrelatedness and synergy of, xii, 99, 129; pedagogy and, 44–45; power of, xiii, 128. *See also* Archibald, Jo-ann
"Strength of a Mother" (poem written for author by her eldest daughter), 72–73
subsistence practices (hunting and fishing): *Alphonse* case and, 9; as closely monitored, 107–8, 113; Colten's experiences of, 100, 101, 104, 106, 112, 113, 114, 123. *See also* fishing; hunting
Sugar Cane (T'exelc; author's home village/reserve community), 12–13, 122; Colten on, 102, 105, 106–7, 113, 114, 118; Elder Jean's stories of family at, 76, 78, 95; English spoken by youth at, 106–7; house of author's grandparents in, 36, 56, 60, 62–63; Mexican visitors to, 105; names of, 12–13; proximity of Williams Lake to, 5, 11, 49; trips to Williams Lake from, 54, 57, 60, 61, 69, 75, 122–23. *See also* T'exelc
support workers, First Nations, at Williams Lake Secondary School: Colten's praise for, 110, 111
survival, Secwépemc: consciousness-raising/decolonization and, 125; cultural identity and, 42–43, 98–99, 124, 128; defence mechanisms for, 10; Elders' teachings/stories and, 42, 99, 124, 131; four Hs (attributes/values) and, 39–40; land/nature and, 43; lessons about, in grandparents' caring for/raising of children, 81; subsistence practices and, 107–8
sweat lodges/sweathouses, 75, 84, 89, 105
sweats, 128; author on, 89; Colten on, 104, 105; Elder Jean on, 84, 87–88, 89
synergy: as principle of Indigenous storywork, xii, 99, 129

T'exelc (author's home village), 4, 5, 28, 36, 48, 124; author's stories of, 50; children as raised by grandparents in, 53; education director of, as gifting author's second Hand Drum, 32; Elder Jean's stories of, 98; as home of author, Elder Jean, and Colten, 7, 14, 100, 126; names of, 12–13. *See also* Sugar Cane
teachings, by Elders/grandparents, xiv, 22, 36, 74, 118–19, 123–24; hospitality/sharing, 38–39, 60, 78; respect, 27, 45, 52, 79–80; and Secwépemc survival, 42, 81, 99, 124, 131; traditional cultural practices, 87–89, 91–94, 97–99, 104–5, 114, 121–22, 126; work ethic, 13, 36–37, 52, 63, 68, 71, 76
technology: end of, as foretold in story heard by Colten, 106; youth and, 42, 97, 112, 113, 115–16, 117, 127
Three Fires Midewewin Lodge, 41
Toosey (Tl'esqox First Nation): Colten's visit to, 103

traditional food. *See* bush (traditional) food
Traditional Knowledge, 23-24; in Elder Jean's stories, 39, 98-99; and four Rs of Indigenous higher education, 23; of grandparents/Elders, 39, 87-89, 121-22, 126; making new meaning of, 44-45; as shared in communal story-telling, 6. *See also* Indigenous Knowledge; intergenerational knowledge transmission; ways of knowing
transportation. *See* driving; horses
trauma. *See* intergenerational trauma
Trent University: Indigenous Studies PhD program at, 21
Truth and Reconciliation Commission of Canada, xiii
tuberculosis (TB): author's mother quarantined for, xv, 5-6, 30, 52, 53, 63, 77; Indian hospitals and, 5-6, 127. *See also* Coqualeetza Indian Hospital; Indian hospitals

University of Alberta: author's participation in summer program at, 19-20, 50
University of British Columbia (UBC), 11, 53, 68; author's PhD completed at, xi, 4, 10, 13, 42-43, 54, 71, 128; Hand Drumming at, 17, 40
University of Northern British Columbia (UNBC; Prince George): author's BA and MA completed at, 70-71
University of the Fraser Valley, Chilliwack campus of, 30
University of Victoria: author's completion of programs at, 70

values, Secwépemc, 9, 11, 22-23, 28, 44; as attacked by external/colonial forces, 22-23, 56, 125-27; as drawn from Colten's stories, 118-20; four Hs as, 39-40; Hand Drum and, 16, 20, 31-35, 128-29; Indigenous Knowledge and, 21-25; as taught by grandparents, 13, 36, 51, 71, 79-80
Vancouver, 83, 109; Aboriginal Friendship Centre in, 10
Vancouver Island University: author as teacher at, 5-6
Vanier, Jean: on belonging, 121

video games: as youth interests/addictions, 112, 113, 115, 116

Walmart, 95, 117
water: as always finding a way forward, 71; as collected for household use, 36-37, 61, 63, 79, 85, 97, 98; as prepared for sweats, 84; as representing emotions, 49; as used to soak/clean animal hides, 29, 114
ways of knowing, Secwépemc: and academia/author's academic journey, 11-16, 21, 25; and author's epistemological knowledge, 45; vs Western worldviews, 16, 25, 129. *See also* Indigenous Knowledge; intergenerational knowledge transmission; Traditional Knowledge
Western worldview: in academia/educational system, 8, 10, 11, 14, 25, 42, 44, 47, 111; vs Indigenous holism, 16, 19; vs Indigenous Knowledge, 20, 22, 24-25, 129; and legality of subsistence practices, 9; and rights of persons migrating to different communities, 94-95
William, Elder Jean (Mumtre Nunxen xw te nek'wests'ut): and announcement of author, 48; author's conversations with, 14, 45; as author's cousin, 77; brother of, 81, 87, 88; as cultural advisor, 83, 89, 99; and encouragement of author, 40; on Secwépemc "return to the land," 21-22, 122; son and grandson of, 80, 87, 88; teachings/knowledge gained from stories of, 98-99
— stories told by, xi, 6, 14, 15, 28, 30, 37, 39, 45-46, 73, 74-99: of author's parents, 77, 86-87, 93, 96, 131; of basket making and gifting, 76-77, 78, 87, 89, 90(i), 91; of childhood/youth, in post-Depression era, 75-76; of Christmas/gift-giving, 95-96, 122-23; of community connections/support, 92-94; of community's self-sufficiency, 75-76, 92; of community's work ethic, 84-85; of cultural/traditional practices, 75, 87-89, 92; of discipline/sharing chores/learning by example, 84-85, 97-98; of Elders being cared for by community, 82-83; of family, 77, 94-95; of family cohesion/strong kinship ties, 75-76, 77-79, 81, 86; of fishing, 83, 84,

87–88, 92–93, 94; of food sharing with those in need, 75, 92–94; of grandparents, 76–84; of grandparents raising grandchildren, 79–81, 82; of grandparents' teachings, 87–89, 121–22; of horses and wagons, 75, 81–82, 84; of hunting, 75, 83, 84, 91, 92, 93, 94; of living with few modern conveniences, 85, 91, 92, 98; of marriage, 76–77, 78–79, 94–95; of mourning customs, 78–79, 87; of practices introduced by Catholic Church, 76, 95–96; of residential school, 86, 92, 96; of seasonal food gathering, 75, 91–93, 94; of sibling relationships, 77–78; of spirituality/church attendance, 85–86
— stories told by, in conversation with author and Colten, xi, 6–8, 14–15, 30, 39, 119–20, 121–28; of Christmas sleigh ride/turkey dinner, 122–23; of place names, as used in Creation stories, 122; of red rock, as marker of Secwépemc territory, 122; and Secwépemc identity, 122–24, 126, 128, 130

Williams Lake: Colten's references to, 101–2, 103, 104, 107, 116, 117, 118; Furniss on, 7, 127, 130; proximity of Sugar Cane to, 5, 11, 49; Secwépemc invisibility/lack of agency in, 31, 127, 130; trips from Sugar Cane to, 54, 57, 60, 61, 69, 75, 122–23

Williams Lake Indian Band (later Williams Lake First Nation), 12–13, 122. *See also* Sugar Cane; T'exelc

Williams Lake Junior High School: author as student at, 65, 66, 67–68. *See also* Columneetza Senior High School; Marie Sharp Elementary School

Williams Lake Secondary School: Colten as student at, 102, 109–10

Williams Lake Stampede, 69, 92

Wilson, Shawn: on "Indigenous" (term), 8; on Indigenous knowledge, 45, 129

Women's Warrior song, xi, 16–17, 71, 126

work ethic: of community, 84–85, 98; as taught by author's grandparents, 13, 36–37, 52, 63, 68, 71, 76. *See also* chores, childhood

Wycotte, Colten: author's conversations with, 14, 45–46, 100; as member of both Chilcotin and Secwépemc families/cultures, 101–3, 107, 119, 122, 126; values drawn from stories of, 118–19
— stories told by, xi, 6, 14, 15, 28, 30, 37, 39, 45–46, 73, 99, 100–20; of alternating visits between two families/cultures, 101–3, 119, 122, 126; of ceremonies external to his cultures, 105–6; of coming-of-age ceremony, 104, 105; of cultural and traditional practices, 101, 104–5, 112; of driving, 117–18, 123; of family relationships, 101–4, 115, 118, 119, 122, 126; of friends, 101, 104, 109–10, 111, 112–13, 114–16, 117, 118; of grandmothers' teachings, 88–89, 114–15; of "hanging out" with his grandmother, 114–15; of hunting, 100, 101, 105, 106, 112, 113, 114, 123; of hunting trip photo, 100–1, 117; of learning/speaking languages, 106–7, 119; of life in Nemaiah, 102, 104–5; of racism, 109; of school experiences/interests, 101–3, 104, 107, 109–12; of shadowing his father on chief's work, 109, 110; of shifting interests/priorities, 112–13, 115–16, 126–27; of spiritual experiences, 105–6; of sports/rodeo, 108–9; of uneasiness living off-reserve, 101–2; of work experiences, 113; of "worry free" childhood life, 101, 102
— stories told by, in conversation with author and Elder Jean, xi, 6–8, 14–15, 30, 39, 119–20, 121–28; of driving, as means of helping others, 123; and emphasis on family ties/connection to two distinct cultures, 122, 126; of hunting trips with grandfather, 123; and Secwépemc identity, 122–24, 126–27, 128, 130

Wycotte family (family of author, Elder Jean, and Colten), 14, 49; Esket origins of, 94–95; fishing ground of, 87–88; property of, as established by Elder Jean's grandfather, 76, 95

Xbox, 115, 116. *See also* video games
xpé7e, 118, 122, 123. *See also* grandfathers

"You Are My Sunshine" (song), 80, 130
Young, Mary Isabelle, 47

youth, Indigenous, 110–16, 118–19, 130; coming-of-age ceremony for, 104, 105; and cultural/traditional practices, 101, 104–5, 112, 123, 126–27; languages spoken by, 66, 106–7, 119; mentorship/support of, 109, 110, 111; movement of, between families/communities, 101–3; nonacademic streaming of, in high schools, 111; and technology, 42, 97, 112, 113, 115–16, 117, 127; work ethic of, 97–98, 126. *See also* Wycotte, Colten

Yuwipi (full moon) ceremony: Colten on, 105, 106

Printed and bound in Canada
Set in Minion by Artegraphica Design Co. Ltd.
Copy editor: Candida Hadley
Proofreader: Alison Strobel
Indexer: Cheryl Lemmens
Cover designer: Alexa Love